YOUR
FIRST
MILLION

Also by Arlan Hamilton

*It's About Damn Time: How to Turn Being
Underestimated into Your Greatest Advantage*

YOUR FIRST MILLION

*Why You Don't Have to Be Born into a
Legacy of Wealth to Leave One Behind*

An entrepreneur's guide

ARLAN HAMILTON

with Rachel L. Nelson

Little, Brown Spark
New York Boston London

Little, Brown Spark
Hachette Book Group
1290 Avenue of the Americas, New York, NY 10104
littlebrownspark.com

First Edition: January 2024

Little, Brown Spark is an imprint of Little, Brown and Company, a division of Hachette Book Group, Inc. The Little, Brown Spark name and logo are trademarks of Hachette Book Group, Inc.

The publisher is not responsible for websites (or their content) that are not owned by the publisher.

The Hachette Speakers Bureau provides a wide range of authors for speaking events. To find out more, go to hachettespeakersbureau.com or email hachettespeakers@hbgusa.com.

Little, Brown and Company books may be purchased in bulk for business, educational, or promotional use. For information, please contact your local bookseller or the Hachette Book Group Special Markets Department at special.markets@hbgusa.com.

ISBN 9780316507967
LCCN 2023939115

Printing 1, 2023

LSC-C

Printed in the United States of America

To Anna,
"…because even when I was flat broke,
you made me feel like a million bucks." (Brandi Carlile)

CONTENTS

Contents

YOUR
FIRST
MILLION

INTRODUCTION

It was May of 2021. I was at Julien's Auctions in Beverly Hills, and I was holding a numbered paddle. The auction? "Iconic Treasures from the Legendary Career and Life of Janet Jackson." Had I ever participated in an auction that didn't take place in an elementary school cafeteria for a new basketball net? Never. Had I studied auction etiquette and protocol the night before on YouTube (and accidentally learned the ages of all of the "Golden Girls" when they started the show)? Of course!

There were more than 1,300 items up for sale, ranging from outfits worn in music videos to personal items and furniture Janet had owned for years. Even though we all know I would have looked absolutely *fire* in her little number from the "If" video, you may be surprised to learn that I didn't have my eye on any of her size 4 clothing. I did, however, have my sights set on another little number, a 1956 Chevrolet Cameo truck that — wait for it — came with a ten-minute phone call with Janet herself, in which she would tell the bidder the personal significance of the truck under NDA! They had me at "You're going to talk on the phone with Janet...." I already had my purple overalls picked out and let my wife know we were moving to a farm so we could drive my new truck around. There was no question: I was bidding on this truck.

Let me be clear here: I knew this was not going to be easy. I found out that *Kim Kardashian* and *Christina Aguilera* were bidding on outfits and there were high-net-worth individuals from all over the world with representatives bidding by phone and online. Plus, the truck was literally called the "centerfold" item, because it was right in the middle of the three-day auction, and it was one of the three most expensive items of the entire inventory. It was also the only item out of more than 1,300 that came with a phone call. In other words, it was on and it was also popping.

If we're being honest, I didn't really think I would win. I had an amount in mind — $100,000 (not including the auction's misnomered "convenience fee") — based on what I could afford and what I thought was worth spending on myself. I was certain I would be outbid by a car aficionado, some rogue Kardashian, or someone buying the truck for a museum. Shortly before the item was to go up for bidding, I took myself to lunch around the corner at a nice restaurant in Beverly Hills. When I came back to the auction room, I asked the person at the front desk how someone would go about paying for an item that was "close to $100,000." She informed me that since most items were going for between $300 and $10,000, people were paying with credit cards. But for high-ticket items (you know, like the ones Kim K and I were bidding on), the auction house would simply take my information and connect with me the next day to make arrangements. At my lunch earlier, I'd been mistaken for a valet for the hundredth time in my adult life, so the irony was even more delicious than the lobster enchiladas.

I settled into a seat and made a couple of bids on gift items for friends to get my auction arm limbered up. It was less intimidating than I thought, so by the time the lot number for Janet's truck came around, it was game on. The bidding started at $55,000. I shot my paddle up. Then on the next bid, someone being represented on the phone outbid me. Then I bid, then they did. Then, less than two minutes from when the bidding started, the auctioneer called for a bid of $90,000. This was near my ceiling, and I knew that if I raised my paddle again, the next bid from my competitor's side would be $100,000, and therefore I would be outbid. So I resigned myself to losing the bidding war and told myself that at least I would walk away with my head held high and my belly full of lobster enchilada. What a story I could tell for the next decade! I proudly and calmly lifted my paddle on $90,000.

What happened next was astonishing: we waited, and waited, but the person on the phone went silent; they did *not* outbid me. To this day, I do not know if it's because they couldn't afford it, didn't think it was worth it, or were simply being kind to the other bidder (aka me), but whatever the case, *boom!* I heard the sound of a gavel hitting the podium, then the word "SOLD!" followed by cheers from the small in-person crowd. I literally jumped up out of my seat like the coach of a ragtag kids' hockey team that had just won the big game. With the inconvenient "convenience fee" added, the total was $114,000!

At that moment I was overcome with emotion. Yes, it was about winning the truck of my hero, Janet. But it was also about the sheer fact of having arrived at this place, at age forty, six years after being homeless and sleeping on the floor of the San Francisco airport. I came to the auction clearheaded after being sober for four years at this point and walked away with the item I'd wanted. I wasn't hungry, hungover, or worried about paying rent or seeing my mom cry because she couldn't keep a roof over our heads. The past five years of hard work and determination — building my venture firm, Backstage Capital, against all odds, going sober after fifteen years of addiction to alcohol, conquering my debilitating stage fright, investing in around two hundred companies led by underrepresented, underestimated founders — the improbability of everything just hit me, all at once.

At thirteen years old, my life was changed by a Janet Jackson concert. It was my first show. My mom was waiting for me in the parking lot because we couldn't afford two tickets, and to say I was excited would have been the understatement of the century. An act of kindness from a stranger meant that my nosebleed seat was upgraded to one in the front row! I would later learn that this stranger was Janet's husband at the time and that this was something Janet liked to do for fans and for herself so she could have the best energy up front. That night shaped me; aside from being the coolest thing that had ever happened to me, and opening me up to the beautiful diversity of the world that I had been mostly sheltered from, it instilled in me the belief that if you're able to do something good for someone else, you should do it. If you're in a place of privilege and you can share that with someone: do it. If you're at the top and you can bring someone with you: do it. I mentioned in my first book, *It's About Damn Time*, that letting someone shorter stand in front of you costs you nothing. That evening steered me in the direction of a career in live music. I couldn't imagine anywhere else I would feel so at home. But the concert did more than that. Janet Jackson has been a huge influence in my life — she was, and continues to be, a role model I needed to see. I'll never forget looking at the crowd behind me from that front-row seat and seeing people of all races, genders, ages, and orientations, singing along to the same songs, united in our adoration of this Black woman. Seeing Janet onstage made me feel good about myself; it gave me confidence and inspired me. It still does.

I don't think I would have launched my magazine, *INTERLUDE* — which started as an online subscription video site one year before YouTube launched and then morphed into a beautiful print version — if it weren't for Janet's inspiration. I'm telling you, from the moment I saw Janet perform for ninety minutes to that sold-out crowd in Dallas, Texas, in 1994, I have wanted to be just like her. No, I haven't been trying to figure out her dance moves —'cause I promise you, none of us want that — but I have been studying her business moves. Janet weaves authenticity and creativity, boldness and innovation, into every new project, every new partnership, every new deal. I learned much of what I now teach from her.

As an adult, I've been lucky enough to have the opportunity to pay all of this forward in many ways. For instance, more than a few times, I've upgraded another Janet fan's tickets at a concert I've attended. I always look for someone in the same nosebleed seats — the only ones I had been able to afford all those years ago. One evening in Anaheim, I chose a mother and daughter who could not have been more excited to join me at fifth row center. Seeing the concert was obviously fantastic, as Janet always puts on an incredible show, but seeing the joy on the faces of these two fans was the best part for me. So winning that auction years later, and then speaking with Janet on the phone about why the truck means so much to her — this was all truly a full circle moment. Plus, as the *Earn Your Leisure* podcast wisely recommends, only buy things you can sell. The truck is an investment.

I am an entrepreneur. Though I began my career in the live music industry, I have been an entrepreneur my entire life, although I didn't always know it. It wasn't something I considered a career path — it was always just part of who I was as a person. Before I started Backstage Capital, I had created a magazine, a blog, a transcription service, and my own merchandise, all with varying levels of success and strife. When I first started researching venture capital, I decided I was going to launch my own start-up: a dating site for women interested in other women. I had even created a beta site for the company — Juliet & Juliet — and I was excited to get it off the ground.

Discovering the start-up and investment community felt like *Wow, I've finally found my people!* The more I learned about the venture capital economy, however, the more I realized that these particular people were predominantly male, wealthy, and white. I was not going to be seen as equal. As a production coordinator in the live touring business, I had worked in an industry dominated by men before, so I knew I was able to speak up and ensure my voice was heard. But the venture capital world was a whole other story, especially considering that I didn't have a degree from a fancy college, a network of people in Silicon Valley, access to a trust fund, or even any experience in start-up investing. I was up for a challenge, I was ready for a fight, but I had wrongly assumed that it would be a fair fight.

I was completely broke when I started Backstage Capital. I'd been dealing with housing insecurity since childhood, and I had been on and off food stamps for most of my adult life. I had hacked my way into a career in the touring music industry, but the nature of this work meant that I would often find myself without any income between tours and in need of a place to stay. In 2015, I crowdfunded money to get into a venture capital class in San Francisco, and once I was there, I put my all into creating Backstage Capital, a venture fund with a thesis of investing in underrepresented founders. This meant that while I was meeting with various possible investors in hotel lobbies and cafés, pitching my ideas and attempting to convince wealthy people that I was a good risk to take, I was spending my nights sleeping on the floor of the San Francisco airport. When I secured my first backer, Susan Kimberlin, I didn't even have my own bank account, let alone a business account. None of that stopped me because I had a vision — I knew that this was what I was meant to do, that empowering and catalyzing underestimated people was my North Star.

Our lives have changed radically over the past twenty years with all of the technological advances that entrepreneurs have made. With each of these advances, we move forward, but we also leave people behind. When one group of people dominates an industry or multiple industries, the consequences can be far-reaching and dangerous. We see this in the medical world, where textbooks for doctors describe the way that a rash looks only on white skin. We see it in the auto industry, where seat belts weren't designed for women's bodies. We see it in emerging technology, with automated soap dispensers and self-driving cars that don't recognize Black skin. What this means is that if we can change who gets to lead, who gets to decide what is a worthy new idea or what to invest in, and who gets to turn those ideas into reality in these industries, we can change the world. This book is for anyone who is interested in getting an idea off the ground, anyone who has found a problem with an established process and knows they could do better, and/or anyone who wants to achieve a lasting legacy of inspiration and representation. I want to guide you in charting your own path to economic self-sufficiency and freedom and help you make decisions that are impactful not just to you and your business but to the people and communities that those in power have historically overlooked. I believe that through entrepreneurship, not only can we change our circumstances — we can change the world.

This book is called *Your First Million* for a couple of reasons. The first is that it's named after my podcast, in which I speak to successful people about their first million something — whether that be one million dollars, one million customers, one million listeners, etc. In speaking to all of my guests, I am constantly learning and updating my worldview and my business strategy. I want to share these thoughts with as many people as possible. The second reason I named my book *Your First Million* is to give you that goal of making your first million. I want every person who reads this book to feel that they have the audacity to aim for that. I don't want anyone to feel like this dream is out of reach for them. We all inherited this world — there is no reason that you don't deserve just as much of it as any other person.

What you won't find in this book is a get-rich-quick scheme. This is not about riches. It's about (as Janet would say) control power and leverage combined. Eighty percent of my life has been spent living below the poverty line. I used to hate money because it made my mom cry, it kept me from having nice clothes, and it meant kids made fun of me. I used to think the best revenge would be to have money. Today, I don't have any reverence for money. It doesn't control me, it doesn't impress me — it is simply a tool. But with that said, it's a very powerful tool and one that is being wielded by only a small percentage of the population. It is my aim to ensure that as many underestimated people get a hold of this tool as possible.

Within the next ten years, I believe I will generate the majority of my wealth. I will use that wealth to catalyze — inspire, build up — as many underestimated people as possible. I intend to catalyze those who will then continue the pattern and invest in their communities. In this way, I want to help create many *mini* empires.

It is important to me for my impact to be far-reaching, to be ongoing, and to live beyond my lifetime. I look ahead and measure success in decades, not in quarters. If you are successful, I believe it is your duty to bring people with you. Never be content to be the one exception. I want to be part of a movement that creates generational wealth in groups that haven't had that before. Just as I invest in founders who are women, people of color, or LGBTQ+, I also want to see more people from these groups becoming wealthy. I want to level that playing field. The best way to begin is to visualize, execute, educate, and amplify.

You don't have to create the next iPhone or Starbucks to become a millionaire. Nor do you need to become a founder or CEO to be an entrepreneur. There are countless ways to be entrepreneurial, and they are all available to you. You can invest in your community or in your home, you can come up with a time-saving solution, or you can invent a product or service that makes your job easier. At Backstage Capital, we have invested in all kinds of companies, all of which have the capacity to create meaningful change: Pandia Health, which provides women access to reliable and convenient health care through telemedicine; Edlyft, which supports students in STEM; Abode (now known as Unreal Estate), which will help you sell your house without the cost of a traditional broker. We are industry-agnostic because we understand that there is more to entrepreneurship than tech, even if the media prefers to highlight the same few social media companies and founders. Success can be derived from so many different industries, in so many different ways.

We are all agents of power. We are all experts in something. We all have the power to make change, whether that be big or small. How can you effect change? What is your calling? And what does success look like to you?

PART ONE

THE AUDACITY OF YOU

The year 2020 threw us all a curveball. In March of that year, the world changed forever. There isn't anything that the global pandemic hasn't affected; nothing is beyond its touch. We had to come to terms with a new normal. The pandemic's indirect effects will continue to impact all of us in different ways. The long-term effect on the economy as a whole is still unknown, but those who lost their jobs, shuttered their businesses, or drained their savings as a result of the pandemic may be feeling the economic pain for some time.

The economic downturn, largely brought on by the virus, has touched every person, every part of society, in some way. Hardworking people have been plunged into unexpected poverty, and as usual, it's the underestimated in society — the minority groups — that have been hit the hardest. Black-owned small businesses had the largest closure rate of any racial group between February and April

2020.* Systemic inequalities mean that prior to the pandemic, Black-owned businesses were in a less comfortable economic position, making them more susceptible to the disruptions caused by COVID-19. Those same systemic inequalities meant that when federal funding for small businesses was introduced as part of the federal American Rescue Plan Act, Black-owned businesses were less likely to apply for grants or loan relief, less likely to have a good relationship with their bank, less likely to be encouraged to apply for government help. Not only that, we watched white tech CEOs, such as Jeff Bezos, become even richer while their employees risked their lives working in warehouses with questionable safety conditions.

Black-owned and minority-owned businesses were also disproportionately affected by pandemic lockdowns due to the industries these businesses were in, as the hospitality and service industries were among the hardest hit. These businesses were also more likely to be located in COVID hot spots.† The House Committee on Small Business noted in their report on Black-owned small businesses that with "the historic barriers to capital experienced by Black

---

* U.S. House Small Business Committee Majority Staff, *The State of Black-Owned Small Businesses in America*, February 26, 2021.

† Claire Kramer Mills and Jessica Battisto, *Double Jeopardy: COVID-19's Concentrated Health and Wealth Effects in Black Communities* (New York: Federal Reserve Bank of New York, 2020).

small business owners and entrepreneurs, state mandated closures in majority-minority industries, while necessary to protect public health, may have caused a perfect storm leading to many permanent closures."[*]

Not only did the failing economy hit BIPOC groups harder, the virus did too. Not because of any physiological condition, but because people identifying as BIPOC were more likely to be in jobs that put them at a higher risk of contagion. Alongside all of this, we watched Black people being murdered by police officers on the evening news, heard awful stories of violence against AAPI citizens, saw disturbing video footage of these attacks on social media, and then witnessed the backlash to the Black Lives Matter movement in the words of those who insisted that "All Lives Matter." (I'm talkin' to you too, Kanye.)

It's been a rough couple of years, to say the least. If I've learned anything from this period of time, it's that nothing is certain. Nothing is immutable, and nothing is unchangeable. Prior to 2020, I couldn't even picture a world where all restaurants, shops, gyms, bars, and clubs would be closed down to keep the public safe. I could never have imagined a nationwide — practically worldwide — stay-at-home mandate. It had to happen to be believed. The

---

[*] U.S. House Small Business Committee Majority Staff, *The State of Black-Owned Small Businesses in America*, February 26, 2021.

pandemic created a situation in which the everyday world was completely destabilized. Activities that had been so normal, that we barely thought about, became a serious risk. Going out became something that we did only if it was absolutely necessary. We had to constantly ask ourselves, *What is really essential?* And although we were all going through the pandemic together, this was where our differences were highlighted. We saw the way in which people's definition of "essential" depended on their job, their housing situation, and their family and care responsibilities. Some people felt stuck inside their homes, glued to a Zoom screen, while others worked in key public-facing jobs and spent even less time in the safety of their homes. Some people were made redundant and lost their jobs, and some couldn't work because their whole industry was shut down.

As painful as it was, moments like these allowed us to reimagine the world. We readjusted our ideas around what mattered. We saw the flaws in our current way of doing things, saw that things needed to change, and identified problems we wanted to solve. We were reminded that nothing in society is "finished," nothing is just "the way it is." Things can change a lot when they have to, so why not try to be the person changing them? All of this was great inspiration for business founders.

While many small businesses closed during the pandemic, there was also a huge increase in applications to start new businesses. According to *Forbes*, July of 2020 saw an increase of 95% in new business applications, compared to July of 2019.[*] This could have been partially due to the complete lack of control that most employees had felt over the past two months. Trust in the government and institutions dropped significantly as the pandemic continued and more industries struggled to survive. Suddenly, more people realized that entrepreneurship provided an opportunity for autonomy and self-sufficiency in a time when everything felt out of our hands.

This boom in entrepreneurship — started during the pandemic but continuing today — is something I'm very optimistic about; innovation excites me, especially when it comes from people who have historically been overlooked. I want to make sure that everyone gets a chance to be a part of the boom, to make the most out of the opportunities it will provide. I want as many underestimated people to start businesses as possible. **I want to see underestimated people elevated to positions of power, and I believe entrepreneurship offers the quickest path to get us there.**

---

[*] Yusuf Berkan Altun, "Pandemic Fuels Global Growth of Entrepreneurship and Startup Frenzy," *Forbes*, April 9, 2021, https://www.forbes.com/sites/forbestechcouncil/2021/04/09/pandemic-fuels-global-growth-of-entrepreneurship-and-startup-frenzy/?sh=6f8c69667308.

CHAPTER 1

SHUFFLING THE DECK

In 2017, only 0.02% of venture capital went to Black women. I am a Black woman. Not only that, I'm a gay Black woman who, when starting out in venture, had no "ins," no college degree, and no money. I quickly learned that I was the opposite of what most Silicon Valley hotshots were looking for and that it was going to be incredibly difficult to get a chance to pitch to anyone, let alone to actually get funding. I started talking to other founders who had similar problems; they — as people of color, or as LGBTQ+, or as women — were just not being taken seriously by the people who had the money and, therefore, the power. Silicon Valley was being advertised as a meritocracy; you have a good idea, you pitch it, you get funding, you build it! What wasn't explained was the huge leap between those first two steps: you have a good idea and then you pitch it. How do you get to the point where you are able to pitch your idea to someone in an industry that relies on "warm introductions"? If you don't move in the same circles as millionaires, how do you find someone to warmly introduce you to the right millionaires who will invest in your company? Even when founders from these underrepresented groups did get a chance to pitch, they were spending 75% of their meeting time providing proof of their worth.

I couldn't understand it; surely if I could see that these founders had something, then the "experts" in Silicon Valley should be able to see it too? And what about me? What about my potential? I was frustrated, and so I began talking to people within the venture capital industry about the bias I was seeing, quoting the statistics I had read. Do you know what I found? Most of them were not only *not* surprised by my numbers, they were not appalled, either. They thought it was "just one of those things." We weren't just underrepresented, we were underestimated. It became clear to me that Silicon Valley duplicated the same systemic racism, homophobia, and sexism that was rife in the rest of the United States and other parts of the world. These powerful people who thought they were on the edge of all the new trends, all the new technologies, the ones who thought they could see the future and control what would happen in the next ten years, based on where they put their money — most of these people were out of touch. They were old-fashioned. They could not see beyond the biased goggles (Google glasses? I digress...) the world had given them.

I began to wonder if I had been thinking about this new business idea all wrong. What if, instead of pitching to venture capitalists and hoping that I could use my powers of persuasion to lock down an investment, I was the one *making* the investments? What if people pitched to *me*? And what if I, understanding that race, gender, and sexuality are not the entire sum of a person, invested in those people who weren't getting the meetings that their straight, white, male peers were? What could that change? I realized that creating Backstage Capital, investing in these underestimated founders, and creating opportunities for people who are underestimated in many areas of life was my calling. This was what I was meant to do.

As the founder of Backstage Capital, what I want is to shuffle the deck so that it's not the same people gaining from the venture capital industry every time. My goal is not to invest in a start-up unicorn that makes one CEO a billionaire and a few other already very wealthy investors even more wealthy. I'm not looking for the one special company that will have a huge IPO, meaning I never have to work again. What I want is to empower as many underestimated people as possible. Let's spread the power more equally! Instead of investing in and helping to create the next one billionaire, I want to inspire the next thousand millionaires. Not only that, I want to see a thousand millionaires emerging from underestimated groups. I want to see a thousand millionaires go on to invest in their own communities, creating generational wealth in communities that have never had it before.

Those of us who have lived in poverty know better than anyone that money is power. We've felt the powerlessness of not being able to change our circumstances. We've seen how easily others have spent money that could have sustained us for weeks. Money gives us more options to positively change our own situation in life, but it's more than that. In the world, as it currently works, money gives you all kinds of other powers — whether it should or not. Extremely wealthy people are invited to be on boards, committees, and task forces and to be government advisers. They have a power that perhaps seems inevitable to them, that feels well-earned — a power that comes from being seen as a successful person in their area of business or from the legacy of a wealthy family. There are so many tables that those of us who are underestimated will never be invited to. Tables we don't even know exist. It's hard to pull up a chair if you can't even find the building. What if some of the most influential tables seated people with a variety of different life experiences? What if we built our own table? What would that change?

More and more we are seeing people use the platforms they have to influence others, and although sometimes that influence can unfortunately be negative, online platforms have lowered the barriers of entry for entrepreneurs, allowing companies to directly engage with, market to, and solicit feedback from their customers and even raise capital through crowdfunding platforms. The proliferation of coding schools and online learning, coupled with no-code tools, makes it cheaper and easier to start companies than ever before.

In fact, the barriers to entry are at an all-time low for underestimated entrepreneurs right now, and that means it's time for me to catalyze as many of those entrepreneurs as possible. It's not just that platforms have given more people access to the tools they need to succeed. It's also that the curtain has been pulled back on what was once an opaque world. We now understand the process and the players. We can learn about other people's journeys through blogs, podcasts (shameless plug: listen to *Your First Million*), case studies, and books. More than ever, we know how much the start-up world is our world too — it doesn't have to be set aside for people who look a certain way or come from a certain school.

In my last book, I wrote that it was about damn time for us to be recognized and for underestimated people to be taken seriously. Now it's about damn time for us to get what is owed to us, what is waiting for us. It's time for you to recognize your worth and center yourself in your narrative. I can't do it for you, but I can give you a guide, and that's what this will be. I want you to spend the next few days reading this book, then take what you have learned and what you are able to do, and use the next five years to set yourself up for the next fifty.

CHAPTER 2

RADICAL SELF-BELIEF

The first step on this journey has to be self-belief. Radical self-belief. In the absence of belief from others, we must have the greatest belief in ourselves. We must be radically optimistic. We must not buy into the scarcity narrative we have been sold. We must never try to be the "only" one — and we need to stop believing there can be "only" one. Radical self-belief means setting goals for yourself that might seem way out of reach. It means looking at the achievements of others and thinking, *Why not me?* And it means concentrating on all the things that you can do and all the talents that you have. Think of it as the opposite of impostor syndrome. Impostor syndrome is a trap and we simply don't have the luxury of time to waste on it. Radical self-belief is the knowledge that whatever you're being paid, it's not enough. Whatever power you have, you can always have more, and there's more than enough to go around. We've been taught that we can't be what we can't see, but I believe this mindset is limiting. We have to understand that we can be *anything*.

I was brought up by my mother, who is absolutely a strong, independent woman. She, and the other formidable women in our extended family, instilled in me a sense of self-belief. The strong, intelligent, kind Black people whom I grew up around ensured that I was proud to be Black. While I didn't see myself or my family accurately reflected on TV or in the media, I *did* see myself reflected in the actual people I was around. It was never a question to me whether we were valuable, whether I was valuable, whether what I had to say mattered. The idea that anybody didn't think that I should be in the room just felt odd — it wasn't logical to me. This sense of self has kept my head above water in times of stormy weather and heavy flooding, and it's given me a strong foundation to build my experiences upon. When I am treated badly, I don't ask what is wrong with *me* — I question what is wrong with the person treating me that way. I was lucky to have good role models in my life, but even if you didn't have those kinds of people, **it's never too late to begin taking yourself seriously.** Build that strong foundation of self-belief, and you won't be swayed by the opinions and whims of others.

There was always something in me that knew without a shadow of a doubt that I would someday be wealthy. It was like a book that was already written, that I had read almost to the end; I knew what was going to happen, I just wasn't sure about the timing. It wasn't a hope or a desire — it was something I just knew, deep down. I have a really clear memory from when I was four or five years old, standing in line outside of day care, waiting to get on a shuttle. At this point, my brother was a newborn, we were a single-parent household, and my mother was only just making ends meet. I remember thinking, clear as day, even before I understood what it meant: *The world is going to know me. The world will know my name.* It was my voice I was hearing, but it was being told to me. I didn't know how the plot would unravel, but I knew this was just the first and second chapters of a much longer book, and there was no possible ending where my circumstances didn't change.

Because of this, I've managed to avoid some of the pitfalls of impostor syndrome. Even when I was thirty-four and still broke, I knew it wouldn't always be that way. When I was trying to start Backstage Capital with no money, no home, and no college degree, I still knew that I was worthy of being in rooms with wealthy people — that there was nothing that made them better than me. This radical self-belief is what kept me going when others might have given up. What I want to be able to do is share it with you all, to give you the confidence to understand how powerful and capable and worthy you are.

Impostor syndrome is something that so many people suffer from. But they don't usually talk about it — because saying it out loud makes them feel like even *more* of an impostor — so they think they are the only ones. That is wrong. Impostor syndrome is systemic. It affects the under-represented more, and we must not fall victim to it. If you haven't seen anyone who looks like you doing the thing you're doing, it doesn't mean you don't deserve to be there or that you won't be as good as the others. It just means you're the first person to step up and have the stars align in your favor, and you're building the stepladder for everyone else like you to climb up and follow your lead.

It helps to remember that many people who are wealthy and successful really aren't that special. They aren't the geniuses we've been led to believe. They've had a head start, yes. Some of them were born into privilege, into wealth, into success; some were given a road map pointing them to exactly where the treasure lay. But innately, there is nothing that makes them better than you or deserving of more than you. You are just as worthy of success, you are just as capable. If you'd been given the same opportunities, privileges, or treasure maps, you could have done just as much. More importantly, you still can. It's not a race. The scarcity narrative encourages the idea that there can be only one winner. But it's false — it's a lie. **There isn't one pot of prize money for us all to fight over; there is room for all of us at the finish line.**

It's not a big surprise that those of us who are underestimated have too often been afflicted with impostor syndrome, given that we are so often seen as impostors by society. Impostor syndrome is reflected back at us, mirrored in the eyes of those who mistake us for the catering staff, or who talk over us in meetings, or who think investing in us is a charitable endeavor. It's not easy to free yourself from the weight of those assumptions and judgments. But you can never control how other people think of you, so the person you must convince of your ability is *yourself*. When other people don't believe in you, you have to believe in yourself for them. You have to take what you consider to be a healthy amount of self-belief and multiply it by ten, because there will always be someone ready to tell you that you are "less than."

As an entrepreneur, and as an underrepresented entrepreneur in particular, there will always be someone telling you that you can't; it comes with the territory, since an entrepreneur's job is to do the things that haven't been done yet. When someone says this to you, directly or indirectly, what they are really saying is "I can't." How could they possibly know what you can and can't do? When I said in 2015 that I was going to invest in one hundred companies founded by women, people of color, or those in the LGBTQ+ community by 2020, people laughed. At that time, this statement was seen as absurd by some; it had been taken as gospel that the reason women, people of color, and LGBTQ+ founders were underrepresented in the start-up industry was simply that there just weren't that many founders in those groups. People told me I couldn't do it, that there wouldn't be enough viable companies to invest in. I said to myself, *It is done. It is already a reality.* In 2018, Backstage Capital invested in its one hundredth company, two years earlier than my estimate. As of May of 2023, I've invested in more than two hundred companies led by underrepresented founders.

Self-belief doesn't magically make all of the systemic issues go away, but it does brace the fall when you're being shoved down. It's like having the right gear for the task. If the task is success, self-belief is essential equipment.

You cannot walk into the world of entrepreneurship — you cannot walk through *life* — thinking that you don't know enough or that you don't deserve to be here. Every one of us deserves to be here. Every person in the United States of America has inherited the same claim to wealth. All of this is ours, and we have to take our share. We must leave behind the scarcity mindset and embrace an abundance mindset. There is enough for everyone, and that includes us.

Does all this sound entitled? Good. What I look

forward to seeing in the future is a lot more entitled Black women. I know entitlement is seen as a negative personality trait, but I would love to see it embodied by people who have been caught up in impostor syndrome for so long. I'd love to see those previously unsure and insecure women stepping forward and saying, "I deserve to be here, I deserve to be invested in, I deserve success, and you will listen to me."

Women especially are taught the importance of being modest, not blowing your own horn. I'm not modest. I acknowledge my wins and shout them from the rooftops, and the result? More than two hundred companies and more than thirty funds led by underestimated people invested in, millions of dollars raised by others with my blueprint, millions of dollars generated by me in revenue (an often forgotten metric), more than a million dollars in scholarships, thousands of people empowered, entire words added to the start-up ecosystem lexicon, and hope for the future. Without a doubt, Backstage Capital has changed the industry. I'm proud of that, and I want people to know about it. Who needs modesty? As Vice President Kamala Harris said, "I'm speaking. I'm speaking."[*]

---

* *The Independent*, "'Mr Vice President, I'm Speaking': Harris Stops Pence Interrupting Her at Debate," vice presidential debate, October 7, 2020, https://www.youtube.com/watch?v=fwW57EGxufE.

CHAPTER 3

EVERYONE'S AN EXPERT IN SOMETHING (INCLUDING YOU)

I started my company Backstage Capital because Silicon Valley executives were hiring and investing in the same kinds of people from the same kinds of schools, and I was tired of it. I didn't (and still don't) believe that being able to afford college was essential to being a founder. Tech lore makes it seem like every successful founder is either an Ivy League graduate or an Ivy League dropout, but in reality that is not the case at all. The mythology surrounding the idea of the "Stanford dropout" has taken a lot of founders much further than they should have been able to go with ideas that weren't worthy of the money invested in them. Access to fancy education doesn't guarantee success.

In my last book, I stated that your *life* is your own education, built for you. Take that education and use the skills you've gained from it, whether that be resilience, thinking on your feet, handling money, or stretching resources. Starting when I was about eight or nine, my mom needed me to look after my younger brother, Alfred, while she worked. There was no babysitter; I knew that if something went wrong, no one was coming to save me. I had to just figure stuff out. From the age of ten, I was essentially a second parent to my brother with my mom; we were leading the household. I learned from her that if things had to get figured out, you figured them out. Thinking on my feet is a skill learned through life experience.

Some of you have qualifications from life that you couldn't get at a business school, and it's time we celebrate that. If you have ever been on unemployment or food stamps, if you've ever applied for a loan, you have experience in filling out financial paperwork. That's a qualification right there. If you have run the finances of a home, working out how much you need to put aside for your dependents, how much you can afford to spend on food and transportation, and how much you need to earn to pay your rent, why can't you run the finances of a business?

We need to dismiss this idea that people living in poverty are ignorant about finance. Only someone who has never felt the anxiety and pain of poverty could think that poor people aren't financially savvy. Why do we think it's only those with an abundance of money who understand it? Those people almost never have to think about it; and when they do, they hire someone to think about it for them! If you've been on the poverty line, you've likely thought about money every moment of every day. You know how much you have in your account, you know the dates your bills need to be paid, you know what percentage of interest you'll need to pay if you borrow money from a lender. You know where to shop on which days to get the best prices.

Being poor is incredibly expensive, and our current financial system punishes the poor for being poor and rewards the wealthy for being wealthy. If you don't have a lot of money, you may end up paying for an essential item through installments, which add up to more than the product is worth. If you're poor and in need of a credit card, the bank will charge you higher rates, as they see you as more of a risk. If you miss one of these payments, your credit rating will drop, meaning you'll be charged even higher rates, making it more and more difficult for you to raise your credit score. So let's stop perpetuating this idea that people in poverty have no understanding of money or that they're poor *because* they lack that understanding.

Here's another thing rich people want you to believe: that you need a certificate or a degree to be an expert. Untrue. I started working at a pizza shop at age fifteen. I understood that there were bills that needed to be paid, that food cost money, and that my mother was already working two jobs. So I helped out. I learned time management, balancing school and my job. I worked every job in that pizza shop, right up to manager. By the time I left, I was absolutely an expert!

Everyone's an expert in something, and that expertise is worth something in the world. What can you confidently talk about for fifteen minutes? What knowledge do you have? What could you teach others? It could come from your experience in your job, your experience as a customer of a service, or your life experience within a certain group. If you're a savvy user of Instagram, TikTok, or LinkedIn, why couldn't you bring some relevant knowledge of how to draw these communities to a business? If you know everything there is to know about a type of music, why couldn't you become a promoter or manage an up-and-coming artist? If you're a fan of a product or business, you likely know a lot about it. You might also have thought of ways in which the product or service could be improved. That user experience is valuable information that companies often pay for.

You are an expert in your own community. You have the knowledge that an outsider doesn't. You can use this information to create something of value. Harness the knowledge of those around you. Ask people what they want and need, what a healthy and successful community would look like to them. Dare to imagine a better world for you and your loved ones. We've waited too long for the same kinds of outsiders to think about us, to consider our needs and our pain points. It's time to create change from within.

More than anything, you are the expert in your own life. There are billions of people in the world, but there is only one you. Figure out where you are, what you want, what your leverage is. If you can't find a business you want to work for, build your own. We who are underestimated, we're natural hackers. It makes sense that we should be successful. Consider your expertise, work out where it is that you can have the most impact and the most influence, and use that. What is the pain point you want to fix? Start asking yourself, *If not me, then who?*

CHAPTER 4

CHANGE CAN HAPPEN ANYWHERE

I think the best ideas come from a founder's personal experience. There is no better research than living through something and no better motivation for solving a problem than experiencing it yourself. If you can see a problem, or a gap in the market, or an improvement waiting to happen, that's where you should start. That was what Linda Hanna-Sperber and Melissa Hanna did when they founded Mahmee, a patient-centric care management platform and one of the companies Backstage Capital invests in. Linda worked in maternal care and often expressed her frustrations with the industry to her daughter Melissa.

There were mothers dying from preventable issues who could have been saved if technology and data were shared and used correctly. For both of these women, the issue was personal. They understood that something had to change, and they set out to change it. They developed Mahmee after just a year and a half of research and development. When pitching their company, it was clear they knew everything about the processes and protocols involved in the maternal health sector. They saw the problem and they were passionate about fixing it. That makes a huge difference to an investor. We need change everywhere. There is no area of life or society that could not be improved, so don't put yourself in a box trying to be what you think of as a successful or wealthy person. You don't have to be the founder or the CEO to make a difference. There are some people who should be creating the newest tech. There are some people who should be creating lifestyle brands. There are some people who should be employee #17 of a fast-growing start-up. All of them have just as much respect from me and should feel just as good about themselves. No CEO or founder or investor works alone; everyone involved in a business has an important role to play. A company will never fulfill its potential if it caters to only one person's life experience.

You need to know a community to know where the pain points lie. A person with a wealthy background cannot easily understand the plethora of problems that comes from being poor. Only people who have experienced poverty truly understand just how expensive it is to be poor. If you have to go into debt to buy something, you can end up paying way more than the product is worth. It is in poverty-stricken communities that predatory loan companies succeed. This is the pain point that entrepreneurs Rodney Williams and Travis Holoway are working to change. They started a company called SoLo Funds, which aims to create financial autonomy for all by providing a way for community members to help one another out with nonexploitative loans. When an unexpected cost occurs, people can turn to one another instead of falling into debt with a payday loan. Their tagline? "In Community We Trust."

You might worry that your idea is so unimpressive or even just nothing — but that idea could be your route to creating change that positively impacts people like you! You don't have to be any particular kind of person; you don't have to look, act, or speak a certain way. You don't have to have gone to a certain school. Those expectations were created by homogenous groups of people within a world with a skewed power balance. There is power in creation, in change, in imagination. Claim that power!

CHAPTER 5

THE AUDACITY TO FAIL

Start-up culture is full of failures. Companies start and end in fewer than two years regularly. Founders give it a go, it doesn't work out, and they close down and take the lessons they learned into the next company they create. Unfortunately, the judgment around failure is not dealt out equally. Parity in Silicon Valley would be the opportunity to fail, and fail again, and then still get some more investors for your third, ultimately better vision. When underestimated founders fail, it's taken as evidence of why we weren't worth investing in to begin with. We deserve the opportunity to fail big and come back stronger.

At age twenty-three, I started my own print magazine called *INTERLUDE*. I had seen some beautiful magazines in Europe while visiting, and I couldn't see anything that fit the same niche in the United States. So I decided to create my own. I was putting together a start-up without knowing it. At the time, I didn't know anything about Silicon Valley or start-ups. I didn't know the jargon or what I was doing. To begin with, I was putting almost everything together myself, doing all of the interviews and the editing. Then I had this thought: *Interview* magazine had people interviewing one another, and that was really intriguing. I started reaching out to some people and asking the featured artists to interview one another. It was a really beautiful and magical experience in a lot of ways. I loved doing the magazine, but it also kicked my butt financially, mentally, and emotionally. It kicked me all sideways and leftways for about five years.

Looking back, I wouldn't change a thing, even though it was really tough, because I learned so much and I was exposed to so much talent. I think it also really developed my chops when it comes to taking a hit. If you're going to start something, whether it be a company, a club, or an event, you have to be able to take a hit. Failure is part of creating anything, and it's never a waste of time. It helps you learn and it builds resilience, and let me tell you, my resilience was just off the charts after creating *INTERLUDE* magazine. What I didn't understand at the time, and couldn't have predicted, was the 2008 economic crash. It wasn't until years later when I was learning about Silicon Valley and read about all the other companies that were ruined that year that I really understood that *INTER-LUDE* closing down wasn't actually the big personal failure that I had thought at the time. Now I can see that *INTERLUDE* was the best lesson in bootstrapping a company anyone could wish for.

I do not let failures — though I don't really consider them failures at this point — get to me because I understand that with hindsight, they have taught me so much. It can be easy to fall into defeatism when you haven't yet had a lot of success. In the moment, you're thinking, *Oh, I'm just not good at this*, and it feels so isolating. But with time, you can look back and see how each failure led you to something new. That's when you can see the skills, the knowledge, and the experience you picked up on the way. Now my failures are other people's inspirations, as well as my own.

Exercises

+ Think through your life so far and make a list of all of the qualifications you have gained from your life experiences. Are you an excellent communicator? Has juggling your work and home life made you great at time management? Do you multitask? Are you good at fixing problems?

- Remember that skills don't just come from workplaces or educational institutions. Life teaches us lessons all of the time. Think about the challenges you have overcome in your life. What can you learn from them?

PART TWO

THE IMPORTANCE OF OWNERSHIP

M any of the wealthiest people in the world started out with generational wealth. All this really means is that their family had money to pass on to them, which gave them a leg up in life. It's a lot easier to start a company, to save for your first house, to start investing, if you begin your career without any debt. Generational wealth is the kind of thing that allows you to go to college, gain a degree — if that's your thing — then head into the workforce with no debt holding you back. Some people will never go to college because it isn't for them, but others never get to really make the choice, because they know that going to college will mean beginning their adult life buried in debt. Generational wealth is also what funds many entrepreneurs' "friends and family round" when they're first setting up their business. It's something that is treated as a normal thing in the venture capital world, which means that many entrepreneurs who don't have it never get their business off the ground. I started Backstage Capital in order to be the "friends and family" for those who were not born with that kind of generational wealth—for those who don't have the kind of people in their lives who can lay down $25,000 to invest in a business that may or may not be successful.

There aren't many people who have done more to advocate for creating a legacy of wealth in the Black community than Dr. Pamela Jolly, the founder and CEO of Torch Enterprises Inc., a strategic investment firm committed to minority business growth and development. For fifteen years, Dr. Jolly has been committed to developing data-driven strategies to ensure that the wealth of underestimated people and their communities is preserved. Dr. Jolly teaches us why it's so important for entrepreneurs, and especially entrepreneurs of color, to own the legacy of their wealth. I first met Dr. Jolly when we appeared on a panel together, and I just had to connect with and find out more about her. I interviewed Dr. Jolly on the very first episode of my podcast, *Your First Million*, and she did not stop dropping gems of wisdom. She explained to me that her company, Torch Enterprises Inc., "stands for passing the torch from one generation to the next to build legacy wealth."* She told me about how working in a corporate

---

* Arlan Hamilton and Pamela Jolly, "Black People Arrived in America on the Balance Sheet…We *Are* Wealth," June 8, 2019, in *Your First Million*, produced by Anna Eichenauer and Bryan Landers, podcast, https://podcasts .apple.com/us/podcast/1-dr-pamela-jolly-black-people-arrived-in-america -on/id1467515562?i=1000441183762.

environment under a fourth-generation banker had made her think about the importance of ownership and equity. She learned that by acquiring her parents' and grandparents' businesses, they could become shareholders, explaining that by doing this, "we could employ our children and we could transform our communities and create the types of programs that would lead to wealth for more of us." Dr. Jolly said that people with generational wealth do two things: "They own things and they cooperate." This part of the book is about the first of those two things.

CHAPTER 6

MONEY DOESN'T OWN YOU

I make no secret of the fact that I have been on food stamps as an adult a few times. I want to make it really clear: there is no shame in using food stamps or taking unemployment. When you're employed, you pay into these programs so that if you find yourself in need of help, you can get it. There is such a stigma about eating off the plate of the hardworking taxpayers, but every day I put money toward other people eating, knowing that if I need it, I could get it too. I understood all of this when I was on food stamps, and I wasn't ashamed, but at the same time I did want my circumstances to change. There were so many times I took the bus in Los Angeles and looked out the window into the distance, knowing I was going back to either a hostel, someone's couch, or someone's roommate's bedroom where the other roommates hated me. I knew something had to change, but I'd been in that situation for so long. Still to this day I have a big emotional reaction to the feeling of hunger pangs. You need hunger pangs so you know when to eat, but it still messes with my head because of how I felt during those years. There were pockets of time throughout my life when I was living a fantastic life, on the road with musicians, living the life I had imagined since I was thirteen and saw my first Janet Jackson concert. But every time I came home from a tour, there were the same money problems. I also had periods of time with friends where money didn't matter because we were all broke but having a great time. I was always the most broke in my group of friends, and as I got older, I felt worse about it. First it was when I was in my early twenties and still figuring out life and careers. Then I was in my late twenties, then my early thirties, and I realized nothing was getting better.

When I hit thirty-four years old, things were even worse financially. I was applying to jobs everywhere, but I was being told I was overqualified for them. I couldn't get a job in retail at all. Oh, I tried, believe me. I tried to be a customer service rep at Airbnb and applied to a hundred other entry-level tech and investment firm jobs, and I couldn't get any of them. I was living and moving around with my mom, as it made sense for us to be together to pool our resources, but then it got to the point where I couldn't bear to see her suffer. Something had to change. I sent her back to our family in Jackson, Mississippi, so I could really go for it.

Eventually, I was accepted into a pilot venture capital education course in San Francisco. The course, mostly taken by millionaires learning how to invest their wealth as angel investors or venture capitalists, brought me into contact with my first-ever investor in Backstage Capital, Susan Kimberlin. I paid for the course by crowdfunding, securing a scholarship, and negotiating a payment plan — I could never have afforded it myself — so the other people there were well outside of my usual social group. Lunches were catered, which was hugely helpful to me, as at that point I was scraping together nickels and dimes for a single Taco Bell item at the end of the day. Every evening I would take a bus back to my Airbnb, try to get a taco, and work on my ideas. Then I would get up the next day, act like that part of my life wasn't happening, and go back to being with these millionaires and trying to pitch this fund that no one was understanding. In September of 2015, when I got the first $25,000 to invest in someone else and the $25,000 to invest in myself and set up shop (thanks, Susan!), I was very clearheaded about it. I decided at that moment that I was never going to be hungry again. I think about that every day with every move I make.

Today, I'm the wealthiest person in my family, but I hope that changes. I live for that to change, for people older and younger than I am to surpass my wealth or to meet me there. All the clichés you hear about money, I'm finding them all to be true — such as if you're a good person, money can help you to continue being good. It's also true that money can't buy you happiness, but it certainly allows you to rent it, and I think those of us who have been on the poverty line can understand that. What's better than being rich is being secure and being okay and knowing I'll never be hungry again. That is the best feeling ever. I have a net worth that is in the top 1% and growing, but in a way it's still just a buffer to keep me the furthest away I can from being hungry.

What's important to me now is that money doesn't own me. I used to hate money, because the lack of it caused so many problems and roadblocks in my life and the lives of those I care about. I wanted to amass a lot of money *because* of that, because I wanted to be on the other side of that. What I've realized now is that money is just a tool, and once you can afford to pay for the essentials — rent or mortgage, dependents, food, health insurance — any money you have left over is a tool you can share with others and use to create change.

What if we were in the position where we no longer had to look at our bank accounts every day (I still do)? If we no longer had to decide whether to eat *or* pay a bill, or worry about how to pay rent? We have the ability to do that if we hack the system in a good way. Too many under-estimated people think wealth is out of their reach, that it belongs to someone else, that it's something we're infringing on. There are people who have been brought up to believe that they are entitled to wealth and power, and the privilege they were born into has helped them every step of the way. But it doesn't have to be that way. *This is our world too.* I'm reading the wills of our ancestors, and I'm here to tell you that this world is just as much yours as anyone else's. Now is your time to claim it.

CHAPTER 7

OWNING THE WEALTH
YOU CREATE

When Hurricane Katrina hit New Orleans, FEMA (Federal Emergency Management Agency) hired Dr. Jolly as a financial expert to help rebuild the city. She explained how the Black community in New Orleans was disproportionately affected by the natural disaster due to the differences in generational wealth that history had dealt them. Dr. Jolly noted, "New Orleans is the oldest inhabited place in the country; Black people were free before they were enslaved. We, at this time of the storm, we had five generations living there. We were three generations in for wealth and ownership...

but the majority of Americans that live there were five generations in."* She explained that it takes three generations to build legacy wealth, and only one generation to lose it. So if you're in that third generation, she said, you're at a tipping point, which means that "when the storm hits, and you're not insured, and you don't have a clear title, there's some issues with cash flow. But when you're fifth generation, it's paid for and it's insured."

So, because the Black community had been able to amass generational wealth for only three generations, they didn't have the same kind of institutional foundations that the white community, five generations into building generational wealth, had. We can see similar patterns with women and the LGBTQ+ community. For a long time, women's access to wealth was dependent on the men in their life, due to laws barring women from owning property, accessing credit, trademarking products, and running businesses. Within the LGBTQ+ community, generational wealth has, in the past, been forfeited for the right to live authentically, because many LGBTQ+ citizens were disowned by their family upon coming out. So some of

---

* Arlan Hamilton and Pamela Jolly, "Black People Arrived in America on the Balance Sheet…We *Are* Wealth," June 8, 2019, in *Your First Million*, produced by Anna Eichenauer and Bryan Landers, podcast, https://podcasts .apple.com/us/podcast/1-dr-pamela-jolly-black-people-arrived-in-america -on/id1467515562?i=1000441183762.

them are just at the beginning of their journey; they're going to be the first generation to pass their wealth on. This is one of the reasons Dr. Jolly believes it is so important that our generation participate in wealth building and creating legacies. We now have the opportunity to do what previous generations could not.

The more underestimated people are empowered to start investing, the more underestimated people will be invested in. In 2021, I started teaching an investor course online, and one of the things I've learned is that so many people don't realize they're already in the position to be an investor. They think they're on the other side of the fence from it, that it's something they can do in the future when they have "made it." But actually, investments can be made with small amounts of money. One way Dr. Jolly advises people to do this is by investing in the businesses where you spend money. So drink your Starbucks, she says, but also own Starbucks stock; or in other words, "Be the owner and not just the consumer." She says that in doing this, you're aligning your investments with the purchase patterns of whatever community you identify with, creating wealth that way.

You don't have to be wealthy to begin building generational wealth. You just have to amend the vision you have of what an investor looks like, what kind of person an investor is.

In the words of Dr. Jolly: "We as African Americans are the only people in America who were first capital before we made capital. And so when we look at business, it can't help but be personal.... We came over here on the balance sheet, and...we are wealth. And we've been creators of wealth from the moment we got here, and so the goal for us needs to become wealth creators for ourselves."

Think about that for a moment. Black people have been creating wealth for this country for generations, but we've been shut out from that wealth and encouraged by the mainstream to think that we aren't, as a group, wealth creators. We've created wealth for so many other people, not just historically, but culturally! How many people became rich from something that our community created? From our music to our fashion to our vocabulary — it's **time for us to own the legacy of our own wealth and understand that it already belongs to us.**

CHAPTER 8

OWNING YOUR PERSONAL FINANCES

In 2019, 59% of Americans lived paycheck to paycheck, meaning they were one paycheck away from homelessness. Only 38% of Americans had an emergency fund.* That's absolutely how it was for me for most of my adult life. Up until I was thirty-four, I didn't make more than $20,000 a year (once as little as $5,000 a year), and it was really hard to save any money at all.

Creating a strong financial foundation for yourself is

---

* Charles Schwab Corporation, *2019 Modern Wealth Survey*, May 2019, https://www.aboutschwab.com/modernwealth2019.

important whether you plan to start a business or you just want to ensure that you have a financial safety net to get you through hard times. The year 2020 was a huge eye-opener in this respect. We learned that you never truly know what's around the corner. So many people found themselves suddenly unemployed as businesses struggled to deal with a worldwide pandemic that none of us could have seen coming. Even those people who thought of their jobs as "secure" realized that in times of crisis, we're all in a position to lose our jobs. Unemployment affected almost every industry, and there were very few "safe" jobs. If you were an essential worker, you were at less risk of being let go or fired, but there was a much greater chance that exposure to the virus would leave you with a huge medical bill or that you would be required to take sick leave or time off to quarantine without being paid. Never mind the fact that the virus could even leave you with any number of ongoing medical conditions that would affect your ability to work and therefore your future earning potential.

Being one or two paychecks away from poverty when COVID hit meant that we were beholden to the government, who ultimately failed us. We needed their bailout, we counted on it, but then it didn't help as much as it needed to because the systemic inequalities and failures of government that created our situation in the first place were still there. If more people were able to have economic independence, we wouldn't have seen so many people suffer as much as they did.

This is why taking ownership of your financial situation is so incredibly important. Whether you're the founder of a start-up, you work for a large company, or you work for yourself, you need to be the CEO of your own finances. To do this, you need to begin with intentionality. The amount of money we have can often feel completely out of our control, with bills increasing every year and wages remaining stagnant. It's important to wrestle that control back.

One way you can take control and create a strong financial foundation for your life is to diversify your income so that you're not completely reliant on one income stream. Figuring this out for myself was huge, especially in the risky industry of venture capital. I've always been curious about other people's income streams, especially wealthy people, who tend to have multiple sources of revenue. I read in a few books and articles that most millionaires have at least seven income streams. Knowing this, I set out to make sure that I was reducing my risk and securing my future by setting up multiple streams of income.

The way people make money now looks a lot different than how it used to. The gig economy (short-term or freelance jobs), zero-hour contracts (jobs in which you are never guaranteed a specific number of working hours), and other flexible ways of working have been both freeing and frustrating for workers. For some, these different systems offer the flexibility for people to work the hours they need when they need to, while for others, the arrangements mean never knowing for sure what their salary will be month to month, so people have to get four jobs to ensure that they'll make enough money to pay their bills.

Some of you may have had multiple income streams for most of your working life. My mother had a couple herself when she worked her day job as a sales executive at a major telecom company, came home and fed her two kids, and then headed out to her night shift at the 7-Eleven. The point of having multiple income streams is that they give you something to fall back on. In 2020, one part of my income came from the release of my first book, *It's About Damn Time*. To launch the book, I had scheduled a tour. I would be speaking in cities all over the United States, celebrating the book, and joining Backstage Capital for a tour in which we planned to give out investments to companies and founders at every date. Unfortunately, the book was set to be published on May 5, 2020, and by the time we got the stay-at-home order that March, I had already been canceling events, as my main priority was always going to be health and safety, for both myself and people coming to the events. It became clear very quickly that the tour was not going to happen. Without those speaking engagements and book sales, I personally lost out on roughly six figures.

If speaking engagements and book sales had been my only income, I would have been completely screwed, but by this point I had seven separate income streams to rely on.

Here are my current income streams, in no particular order:

1. My **salary** as the managing partner of Backstage Capital and the owner of ArlanWasHere LLC. Salary is the main source of income most of us count on to pay bills and buy food, and it tends to be the one that's most consistent from month to month. But that salary keeps coming in only so long as some company keeps paying it. As we've seen, companies can go out of business, downsize, and let people go. If you're ever in that position (I have been!), you'll be happy to have another income stream to fall back on, even if it's only enough to cover the cost of gas to get to your next job interview.

2. My second income stream comes from my **publishing deals.** This includes the advance that I receive when I make a book deal, which usually comes in four parts over approximately two and a half years. Once the book is released, as long as I sell enough to earn my advance, I then receive a percentage from book sales. This might be a small amount of money coming in a bit at a time, but it could be an income stream that lasts for decades. The more books I publish, and the more

books I sell, the larger this income stream grows over time. Indie publishing can be a great option for some people — I'm a big fan, and it is something everyone should contemplate, considering how hard it can be to get a book deal from a publishing giant.

3. Return on **investments** (ROI) and "carry" (short for "carried interest") is another source of income that, over the next few years, just may turn out to be the largest. I make investments via Backstage Capital's assets under management (AUM) and have a significant ownership in the umbrella entity that manages these investments.

4. **Speaking engagements** form a large part of my income, which is why the cancellation of my tour was such a blow. However, once we pivoted to online events, I've continued to book interviews and fireside chats. I'm now back to generating more than one million dollars most years in speaking fees alone, in person and virtually.

5. **Media deals,** which cover anything from television to podcasts, etc. My *Your First Million* podcast is a great example. So is my fictional soap opera podcast, *The Valley.*

6. In 2020, I launched my first course, How to Raise Start-Up Capital, which created another income stream of **courses and digital products.** I'd never created a course before, but I knew I had the expertise

and the knowledge to create something that would be beneficial to those who wanted to learn. Not only that, I knew that my expertise was worth paying for. I loved building the course, and after such a positive experience, I knew it was time to start Arlan's Academy. I could create and host more courses led by all the incredibly talented and knowledgeable people in my network. Not only is it a great resource for founders, it's been a great source of learning for me too.

7. Another revenue stream is **consulting.** When I first started researching what the whole venture capital thing was all about, I couldn't have known that people would eventually be paying me for my expertise, but that's exactly what has happened. My time, experience, and knowledge are worth money, and the time I spend working as a consultant gives me more experience, further adding to my value while also making me money. It's a win-win.

For some of you, seven income streams might seem like a reach, and I understand. I barely had one income stream for the first thirty-five years of my life! Try adding just one new income stream to start, and see if you can add more over time. Think about a field where you're an expert. Is there a way to monetize that expertise? For example, let's say you know a lot about a particular area of business, such as IT or marketing. You could begin by building a free online course on this subject and encourage people to take it and leave reviews. You could then use this feedback to improve your course and eventually look to sell it to one of the many course websites available. Or let's say you're super detail-oriented and organized, making you great at administrative tasks. If that's something you enjoy, advertise your skills and see if you can put in a few hours a week as a personal assistant for someone. We all have so much life admin that we have to deal with, and some people really despise doing it, so you may find yourself in high demand. This is one of the reasons I launched Runner, a job matchmaking service, at hirerunner.co.

You should also ask yourself where your skill sets intersect. For example, you may be an accountant with a separate revenue stream coming from Etsy sales, because it turns out that not everyone who is good at figuring out profit margins can sew as well as you can. Some of the income streams will definitely take more work to begin with, and it may take some time to see a big return. But remember, you're building an income stream for the future, and that can be worth the investment of time.

I want to make it clear that I am not suggesting you try to monetize all of your hobbies. Sometimes you do things just for fun, to relax, and you don't want to feel like you have to do that thing to a sellable standard. You need to be free to pursue things that may not be your strength but you enjoy anyway! I don't want you side-hustling your way to stress and burnout. So you have to know where to draw the line. Life is full of trade-offs, and you have to be able to ask yourself whether the money made is worth the stress involved. If it's going to take up all your spare time to make something you can sell only at a low price point, it's probably not worth it. Do look out for those opportunities to diversify your income with as little drain on your free time as possible. Remember, an extra revenue stream isn't another salary, so it doesn't need to be another full-time job. It could be something that you do only a couple of times a year; that's still a couple more opportunities each year to make money.

For some people, adding new revenue streams won't be possible right now. That's okay! It may be that between your day job and all your other responsibilities, you don't have time to create another revenue stream. But this is something to keep in mind and to work toward.

When it comes to money, I'm a big proponent of autonomy and accountability. That doesn't mean you can't work for someone else — it means you are constantly and confidently taking ownership of your life and steering your life, not letting life happen to you but participating in navigating the direction of your life. The wonderful thing about this is that you can start doing it — taking life by the horns — in this moment. That means taking an audit of your resources, an audit of your desires, hopes, and aspirations. *What do you have today, what do you want to achieve, what do you want to have? What tools and resources will you need to get from where you are to where you want to be?*

CHAPTER 9

OWNING YOUR COMPANY

L et's talk about Mark Cuban. My collaborator, friend, and sole limited partner in the $6 million Arlan-WasHere Investments, a fund within Backstage. Mark is an embodiment of the power of ownership. He created and owned his own companies and sold them for substantial wealth. His first venture sold for a staggering $20 million, and his second, even more impressively, sold for billions. This ownership has given him tremendous power and leverage. It's a testament to why I stress the importance of ownership to all entrepreneurs. Mark's success isn't just about the monetary gains but about the influence, political power, and quality of life he has managed to cultivate.

This is what I want for you. This is what I want for all of us. When you own, you control. You decide what impact your work will have in the world, how it will shape society, and how it will contribute to your legacy. That's why the ArlanWasHere Investments fund is so special to me. Mark and I built it with the core intention of fostering this culture of ownership, particularly within underrepresented founders. This is about wealth, yes, but it's also about leveling the playing field and equipping more people with the means to bring their visions to life.

One of the best ways to cultivate power and income and begin building your legacy is through ownership of your own business. But as the old saying goes, it takes money to make money, and unless you are independently wealthy, you may not be able to afford the cost of getting a new business off the ground. This is where people like me come in. As a venture capitalist, I receive thousands of applications for funding every year. I'm often asked, "What do you look for in a founder? How do I get investment in my company?" There are lots of ways to raise money for a company, and it's important to consider them all before you take on any investors. Never forget that anytime anyone invests money into your company, you are going into business with them. For this reason, it's important to really consider not only how much investment you need but *who* you take investment from. Would you go into business with just anyone? No. If you already know them, you'd think long and hard about how going into business would affect your relationship. If you don't know them, you'd want to find out a lot about them before taking such a big risk. It's the same with investment.

The reason your source of funding is important can be summed up in one word: equity. Your equity is how much ownership you have of the company. Every time you accept money as investment, you give away a piece of your equity, or potential future equity, and you need to look ahead and think about whether the money being offered is worth what you are giving up in terms of ownership. If you engage in many fundraising rounds, the ownership of your company will be split so many times that you no longer own the majority of your company. This means that you are no longer able to make decisions about your company without consensus, and you no longer receive the majority of the returns down the road if your company is bought by a larger company or a group of investors (what's known as an exit).

When it comes to raising capital, there are multiple routes you can take. Some are more accessible, some more risky, and some more conventional than others. There's no right or wrong way to fundraise; it depends on your financial situation, your business plan, and your goals. A lot of the time, it's also dependent on your network, which is one of the reasons that underestimated founders have struggled to get a foot in the fundraising door in the past.

As I mentioned earlier, the first stop on the fundraising journey is often the **friends and family round,** which basically means that you ask a certain number of your friends and family members to invest in your idea. The amount raised at this stage varies, depending on how many of your friends and relatives want to invest in your idea and how much they can afford. Unsurprisingly, this is where we see the stark difference between underrepresented founders and founders who come from wealthy families or who have connections to other people with wealth. Some of those founders have raised hundreds of thousands of dollars at this stage just by pitching to the people in their network who have capital to spend. For most of us, though, this is an impossible ask. At the start of my journey, I sure didn't have any friends and family who could casually invest $10,000 into an idea, let alone ten of those people.

Beyond being inaccessible for many, the friends and family round is also risky. When you ask an investment fund to finance your company, they absolutely know what they're getting into. They crunched the numbers, they know the odds, they are prepared for the risk. They have little emotional connection to you, and you have little emotional connection to them, besides wanting to make them their money back. If you are going to ask for investment from your friends and family, consider this: Do you want to be responsible for someone you love losing their life savings? If you take this route, you must be clear with your network that more than 50% of start-ups fail in the first two years, so statistically, the odds are against them. For this reason, it's important not to take too much money from one person. Spread out the risk and make sure that those who invest can actually afford to lose the money.

What I would like to see in the future is more underestimated founders being able to use this kind of fundraising *if* they choose to. The more successful underestimated founders there are, the more those founders can invest in other underestimated founders and tip the scales in terms of who has access to this type of network.

After the friends and family round, founders will typically turn to **angel investors:** people who have a certain amount of personal capital they would like to invest, usually in exchange for an ownership stake of anywhere between less than 1% to 10% of the company. Angel investors must be accredited, which means (according to SEC criteria) they either have a net worth of $1 million, earn a minimum of $200,000 per year, or earn a minimum of $300,000 combined income with a spouse. When working with angel investors, it's important to make sure that you have a good founder-investor fit. Don't blindly take money because it's offered and you need it. Look into the person's investment philosophy, their values, their agenda. If you are not aligned on these things, you will not be aligned on the important decisions that impact your business.

Another type of investor is known as a **family office.** These consist of either one family or a group of families who are very wealthy and have hired someone to invest their wealth for them and then manage those investments. Generally these family offices aren't talked about much, and you would need a very warm introduction to get in touch with one, so few underrepresented founders end up taking this route. The positive side of family offices is that they can make decisions and write checks very quickly, and those checks can be as large as those signed by a venture fund. This is another route that I hope to diversify in the future by creating generational wealth in Black communities. I hope to see many more Black family offices created and to see them investing in underestimated founders.

The most well-known type of start-up investment is **venture capital (VC).** Venture capital funds invest the money of other high-wealth individuals who have invested in their fund. For this reason, venture funds also do their own fundraising. You may be able to raise a large sum of money through the venture capital option but often for a high price in terms of your equity. There is a structure to venture fundraising; you begin with pre-seed funding, then seed funding, and then series funding: A, B, C, etc. A seed round is essentially just a round of fundraising, and the more rounds you have, the more you are diluting your equity. You also have a lot more people to answer to, and the expectations of those people will be higher because more money will be at stake. When a venture fund invests in your company, they don't hope to just make their money back plus a little extra — they generally expect you to make ten times their investment or more. They will expect you to grow the business rapidly in order to do so. For some venture capitalists, anything less than that is perceived as a failure.

Almost 50% of all public companies are venture capital–backed. But what most people don't realize is that public companies are only a small slice of the market. In fact, less than 1% of all US companies are publicly traded, which means that only a small percentage of companies overall receive venture capital funding. But because venture capital is the most well-known of the fundraising options, receives outsize attention in the media, and is glamorized in movies and TV programs, it would be easy to assume it is your only choice when you're starting out. It is really important to understand that venture capital is not the only way to fund your business! It is one option, and it may even be the right one for your company, but it is not the only option. When you're starting a company, it is my advice that you hold out as long as possible and explore as many other options as possible before looking to venture capital for money. If you start asking for huge checks at the get-go, you will likely need to continue in that fashion in order to grow at the rate your investors will want you to grow. This means that you're going to be left with very little equity and a lot of people to answer to. You could even be fired as the CEO of your own company if your equity is too diluted, so if control is important to you, be very careful about going this way.

Even though I'm a venture capitalist, **bootstrapping** is my favorite kind of fundraising. Bootstrapping involves relying on sources of income that you own — such as revenue from sales and your own savings — rather than outside investments to fund your company for as long as you can. Bootstrapping simply means funding a company without taking any outside investment, which allows the founder to have as much control over their business as possible and to hold on to their equity for as long as possible.

So much of what we read about start-ups in books, business press, and other media creates the impression that from day 1, the primary job of a founder is to raise capital. This is misleading. There are plenty of other things a founder can — and often should — do to launch and grow their business, other than court investors and raise money. So before thinking about how quickly you can raise a round on day 1, think about your first customers, your business model, creating the best possible product, and what kind of team you want to have sitting next to you on day 1,000.

Bootstrapping makes it easier to stay true to your original ideas and to be beholden to no one but your customers and yourself. As the founder, you should be the person who knows the most about your business and your industry. This means that if you get to a point where you can see that the marketplace is changing or that something you're doing isn't working and you need to pivot, you can go ahead and do that without having to get permission or buy-in from investors. With no investors to answer to, you can spend less time selling investors on your vision and more time talking to your customers, fine-tuning your product, and working on making that vision a reality. I've spoken to so many founders who have had to ask for permission from their larger investors before they make a decision that, in my opinion, they shouldn't even need to ask about. Never forget that you are the expert in your company.

When you take venture capital, you immediately have a boss. But if you're an entrepreneur, you probably prefer *to be your own boss* — that's partially why you got into this, right? With venture capital, you are beholden to other people's ideas of success. You are held to someone else's benchmarks, and if you don't grow your company tenfold, it's considered a failure, even if you have thousands of loyal customers. Can you imagine if we held all other businesses to this standard? "Oh, you didn't make more than ten times the amount of money you made last year? What a failure." The bottom line is that you're the founder, which means you're the one who gets to decide what success looks like.

What I think a lot of people miss in my story is that while I've raised a few million dollars from investors and generated millions of dollars in revenue since I started Backstage, I've also bootstrapped companies to keep the lights on. When I started my podcast *Your First Million*, I was offered money, which I turned down. I wanted to ensure the podcast remained exactly how I wanted it to be.

Bootstrapping can mean having to scrimp and save, but you get to retain your ownership along with the freedom to make mistakes, learn from them, and move on. It takes longer, of course, but the slow pace allows you to grow intentionally and iterate as you go, rather than try to scale as quickly as possible — often before you're ready — to meet some impossible standard of growth. Plus, in the extra time you give yourself to learn the ropes, you're also leveling up your talent. I think we need to start changing the way we look at outside capital as being the best source of funding.

Blended Designs began as a T-shirt business in 2014 but really took off in March of 2017, when founder Casey

Kelley was on medical leave from her salaried job. She had a second income stream from her T-shirt business, but the profit margins were very low. One day her eight-year-old son, Carter, came home from school and said, "Mommy, I have an idea for the business. I want a bag with my face on it."* Casey's day job was in consumer insights and analytics, so she was able to use those skills to research what her son was asking for. She found that fewer than 2% of the bags in this market depicted characters of color. This was a gap in the market that she knew needed to be filled — children of color deserved to have the option of buying a character bag with someone who looked like them on it. Blended Designs began producing backpacks with a range of characters and the slogan "I Can Do Anything." Even Casey could not have predicted how high the demand for this product would be, and she initially struggled to fill all of the orders that were made. The backpacks were branded "1954 by BD," a nod to the 1954 *Brown v. Board of Education* ruling that desegregated schools in the United States and to the fact that Blended Designs aims to desegregate the back-to-school category in retail. Within four months of

---

* Arlan Hamilton and Casey Kelley, "Blended Designs—How Black Representation Turned into $1M in Backpack Sales," June 9, 2020, in *Your First Million*, produced by Anna Eichenauer and Bryan Landers, podcast, https://podcasts.apple.com/us/podcast/your-first-million/id1467515562?i=1000477385173.

launching the 1954-branded backpacks, Blended Designs pulled in a quarter of a million dollars in sales, with Casey and her husband, Harvey, running the company full-time.

At first, they were a mom-and-pop shop, working from their home, using their shared bank account for the business as well as their personal funds — as many entrepreneurs do when bootstrapping their company. Then, in 2018, they were approached by Walmart, who wanted to sell their products online before stocking them in their physical stores, but the Kelleys didn't have the inventory or any way to produce it at the scale required. At this point, they knew it was the right time to look for outside investment, and they made a deal with a minority-owned venture capital firm in Jacksonville, Florida, where they lived. This was the turning point for Blended Designs that allowed them to reach a million dollars in sales in 2019. When I spoke to Casey in 2020, Blended Designs was on its way to pulling in another million dollars that year, even with the pandemic closing schools down for long periods of time.

Another key milestone for Blended Designs came when the pandemic hit. Suddenly, kids had to start wearing masks, and as a savvy mom, Casey knew that just like everything else kids wear, they would want their masks to be fun. Not only that, but there just weren't as many masks for children available, so she had spotted another gap in the market. In 2020, Casey announced Blended Designs would be producing masks printed with their ten characters and their "I Can Do Anything" slogan. She expected around five hundred sales over the next couple of weeks, but once again the response was huge, with thousands of orders pouring in within the first few hours after the masks were announced. The pivot from backpacks to masks was a bit risky, but it worked, in part because Casey and Harvey bootstrapped so much of their business in the early days and still owned the majority of Blended Designs. This meant they were able to be nimble and make the important decision to pivot without having to ask for permission from a board of investors, which would have slowed down the process so tremendously that the moment to strike would have been lost. This is where the importance of ownership becomes clear.

Bootstrapping won't always be possible, especially if your product is expensive to make, your profit margins are low, or you don't have savings you can afford to pour into your business. But here are some ways you can begin: Make a list of your monthly expenses and see what you can eliminate and reduce. Do as much of the work as you can yourself before hiring other people or spending money to outsource various services. There are so many resources out there now that can help you do things yourself cheaply, such as software that helps you build a website for yourself easily, without needing to know how to code; online courses that can teach you how to manage your brand; and social media platforms that allow you to get to know your customers — and what it is they want from you.

Consider your assets and revenue streams. Are you able to monetize some of your skills, perhaps as a consultant for other companies? Can you tap your network to negotiate a skill swap with another founder? Can you afford to experiment with pricing and packaging to improve your profit margins? When we see representations of startups in pop culture, it's often the same storyline: "I quit my job to pursue my dream!" That's great, but if you have a steady job, you should think hard before you quit your main source of income. If you have the kind of job where you can slowly reduce your hours, that would be the best option. Consider that the first investor in your company could be your day job.

Suneera Madhani, cofounder of Stax, a tech company that "radically simplifies the payment ecosystem,"[*] didn't know anything about venture capital when she began building her company. So before she took any money from venture capital investors, she participated in pitch competitions. She would walk in, pitch her business idea, and walk away with a check. She raised $200,000 for Stax through pitch

---

* Robert Reiss, "CEOs Share Insights on Purpose-Driven Companies," *Forbes,* June 15, 2022, https://www.forbes.com/sites/robertreiss/2022/06/15 /ceos-share-insights-on-purpose-driven-companies/?sh=1af2c8621e18.

competitions alone. This is an amazing way to source a large amount of money that doesn't cost equity or come tied to a contract.

Whether you decide to take venture capital or not, it's always important to remember that while money often does equate to power, it's more important to be in control. This means never being dependent on one investment. Backstage Capital has had investments fall through at the last minute more times than I can count. If we'd had no plan B for those times, we never would have been able to continue with the company.

Venture capital is, of course, a very useful fundraising tool, but it is best when used carefully, at the right time. The longer you can bootstrap your company, the less equity you are giving away. You want to be at your strongest point, where an injection of capital will do the most for your company, before you approach investors.

If and when you do get to that point, you need to consider what you're gaining and what you're losing. It's really important to have a good idea of your own value so that you know when a deal is good for you. You will need to be aware of the value you've created so far (through validating your idea and the research you've done around it, as well as the level of product or team already built) and the market for deals in your space. As with every part of starting a company, research is key!

Another alternative to taking VC money is to apply for a spot in an **accelerator,** which is a structured program designed to help accelerate a start-up early in its development (or an **incubator,** which is aimed at founders even earlier in the process to help them bring their ideas to life in a controlled environment). Companies accepted into accelerator programs are usually given "a seed investment," anywhere between $20,000 and $125,000, in exchange for a portion of their equity ranging from 2% to 10%. Accelerators usually involve some aspect of mentorship from the organizers, which can be extremely helpful. It's also a good way to network with other founders and meet people in the ecosystem. If you're applying to accelerator programs, make sure that you have done your research first. Find out how much equity you will be giving up and what their terms and conditions are. Will you need to relocate? Are you required to go into fundraising rounds after the program, or can you opt to bootstrap your company? What perks do you receive? Who are the mentors? Find out how other founders who were accepted felt about the program!

Another way to bootstrap your business is through **debt:** specifically, through bank loans or SBA (Small Business Administration) loans. You can also use debt as a way to protect your ownership stake in venture capital funding. This is when a venture capitalist gives you a loan and doesn't take equity in your business. Instead of expecting payment when the company eventually is sold or goes public, the lender issues a note with a date for repayment. They can also use a convertible note, which will state a date or milestone at which the debt will be exchanged for equity. It's important to remember that no money is free, so no matter what, you'll always be incurring some kind of debt. I think if you are very serious about your company, you have a steady revenue stream, you know you can pay the money back, and you have done your research and understand the ramifications of taking on debt, this can be a legitimate way to raise money for your company. However, most of the time you won't be able to take on enough debt to cover everything, so loans are usually used just to supplement another kind of funding.

It's also worth mentioning **grants** at this point. Depending on the focus of your business, you may be eligible for research and philanthropic grants. Usually these would be given early on in the start-up process, so again, do your research and see if you can benefit from any of these.

A favorite way of mine to raise money is **crowdfunding and/or equity crowdfunding.** Crowdfunding involves your community (customers, new fans, etc.) giving small amounts of money to a project to ensure that the project can go ahead. Usually you will set a fundraising goal, and if you reach it, everyone who contributed gets something in return, such as a T-shirt, a public thank-you, or early discounted access to the product or service. Some examples of crowdfunding sites are Indiegogo, Kickstarter, and Seed&Spark, which is a Backstage Capital portfolio company. You may well have contributed to a crowdfunding campaign yourself!

With *equity* crowdfunding, instead of getting only a T-shirt or a thank-you, those contributors get a tiny piece of the company. Prior to the JOBS (Jumpstart Our Business Startups) Act, which passed in 2012, only accredited investors could invest in start-ups. But now almost anyone can browse crowdfunding websites and invest in companies. This can be a great way to raise some capital for your company without giving away too much equity, and it's also an opportunity to test the market, as you're more likely to be interacting with people who will be your customers. Some examples of equity crowdfunding sites include Republic, Wefunder, and SeedInvest. One advantage to equity crowdfunding is that it allows people who really care about the company to own a part of it, making them literally invested in its success. Gimlet Media, the company and podcast network that produced *StartUp*, a podcast that featured me and Backstage Capital in a six-part series in 2018, used equity crowdfunding as part of their capital raise. They crowd-equity-funded the last $250,000 to give their listeners a chance to be owners, meaning that when it was sold to Spotify in 2019, those crowd investors made upside.

The downside to equity crowdfunding is the amount of information you have to make public. It requires a lot of paperwork, and you will need to show all of your financial information publicly. You'll need to make a really strong case for why people should invest in you, so ensure that you put your best foot forward when you begin this process. Before applying to use a certain platform, get in touch with the fund organizers directly and ask what you'll need to disclose in order to use their site. Always know what you're getting into!

In September of 2021, I launched my company Runner, which seamlessly matches fractional and temp-to-hire operations talent with inclusive start-ups that have one to one thousand employees. I decided that I was going to bootstrap Runner as far as I could, and not only that, I was going to do it in public. I wanted complete transparency. If it failed, I wanted people to see why and to learn from it, and if it was successful, I wanted people to see that too and understand that they could do the same thing one day. So far, I have raised $3 million through angel investors and one seed round. After seeing the power of raising through crowdfunding and what that could mean for the future, aside from the positive effect I believe this will have on the generational wealth of underestimated groups, it has also given me a sense of mental freedom.

Taking all of this into account, you may wonder why

I'm a venture capitalist. The answer is simple: because venture capital is powerful, and we deserve to see ourselves represented there. As Ollen Douglass of Motley Fool Ventures pointed out on my podcast (episode 48), out of the ten most valuable companies in the world, seven of them are venture-backed. The three that aren't were created prior to venture capital existing. These companies are driving industries, and it's important that underestimated people are a part of that. Venture capital can help people create generational wealth and can help create economic equality. If we cannot play a part in controlling economic resources, we're going to continue to live in a racist world where we routinely see the public execution of people of color on television.

There is not one right answer to the question "How should I fund my business?" The right funding route for you will depend on a lot of factors, including expenses, how big a team you need, your price point, etc. These should all be considered when deciding which type of funding is right for you. Your company may have high overhead costs that require a large investment up front, or you may have something you can bootstrap to a million-dollar valuation. As always, the most important thing is to do as much research as possible. Find out who the players are, what they're offering, what you're giving up, and what it means for the future of your company.

CHAPTER 10

OWNING YOUR PROFITS

When you run a venture fund, you usually receive a management fee. This fee comes from the assets under management (AUM), and it's usually around 2% of the total amount invested in the fund. If you have a $20 million fund, with $20 million committed every year, the management fee would be around $400,000. That's enough to employ maybe one or two people and then pay the third-party vendors who are helping with legal, accounting, etc. Sometimes those legal and accounting costs, as well as the fund formation expenses, are covered by the fund outside of your management fee, but in general it will all come from the 2%. So $400,000 is a good amount of money to run a solo fund or run a fund with a friend. You both get a good salary that can pay the bills, maybe you lease a coworking space, and you're off to the races.

Backstage Capital has never had that type of money. The capital raised for Backstage was raised in small increments, usually $25,000 at a time, and we never had a committed investment that we could count on year after year. Because our fund was small, the usual 2% given for the management fee didn't cover the costs of running the fund. In some of our earlier funds, when we raised one million dollars, I got a small fee, but I took it up front — a few thousand dollars at most — so it really didn't do the job that a management fee is supposed to do.

In larger funds, especially hedge funds or private equity funds, the managers will sometimes sell percentage points of their profit share to cover their operating expenses. In these cases, they tend to have a lot of money under management, and they know where things are going moneywise, but they're looking to liquidate a little bit earlier. One example of this is Robert Smith, who has sold hundreds of millions of dollars' worth of his own upside to a firm called Dyal Capital Partners. So it happens every once in a while, but it's not the norm. Usually, that management fee would cover the expenses. It's there to prop up your company.

Because the management fee for Backstage Capital

couldn't cover our expenses, I had to be creative, flexible, and forward-thinking to keep the company running. So as soon as I started raising capital, I started selling off parts of my own profit share, my carried interest (aka carry). Even back in 2015, I knew that Backstage was going to become something big — I knew it was worth something. I knew this because I wouldn't have it any other way. But I also knew I had expenses to pay, so I decided to sell a sliver of my future upside. Each $25,000 or $100,000 infusion helped me keep the lights on at Backstage.

By the time I looked up in 2018, I realized I had sold too much of my carry. I don't regret it, because it kept me in business, but as Backstage started hitting major milestones, such as growing our portfolio to one hundred companies and hiring more amazing staff, I began to feel disheartened by the fact that I had had to give up so much of my future profit to get us to this point. Things were really starting to move forward. We were growing. We had brand recognition. And I knew some of the companies we had invested in were going to do big things. I hated the fact that I had had to give up so much so early. I also knew that the next few years were going to be tough if I was already at such a loss. I started thinking about going back to some of those investors, especially the ones who had the larger amounts of capital (there were one or two who had an outsize portion), and asking to buy back some of that carried interest. The problem with that was that I still didn't have the money to buy it back yet.

Fast-forward to 2020. The pandemic has hit, and like many companies, we had to lay off some staff. We were running on fumes, not for the first time, and we had to decide what was next for us as a company. Did we want to keep our amazing portfolio but work other jobs day-to-day? Or was there another way to keep things going? I thought back to Robert Smith and those other hedge fund managers who had sold a portion of their carry to a large institution in exchange for a minority stake in their company. I'd done the same thing on a smaller scale and regretted it, and now here I was, having to do it again. So I decided to do it differently this time. I wanted to do it in a way that felt like a win for more people — in a way that would deliver those early investors even more value, at least on paper, than they had received before, while also getting new investors into Backstage. I started thinking about crowdfunding — not for the fund itself but simply to finance the management of the fund.

In March of 2021, our crowdfund launched, and we restructured. When the dust settled, our early investors had more value than they previously had had. I was still the majority stakeholder in my company, and we now had nearly seven thousand new investors who would also benefit. I finally felt like things were balanced and fair again.

This is why I'm such a big believer in second chances. I'd given myself a chance to correct my earlier mistake, and it paid off. Sure, I could have just settled for being a minority stakeholder in the company I built. Instead, I found a way to keep the company afloat without shortchanging anyone, including myself.

CHAPTER 11

OWNING YOUR EXPERTISE

Up until 2017, I had severe stage fright. I was being told I could be making money as a paid speaker and I was being offered gigs, but I was too scared. I now speak to audiences of up to twenty thousand people. I'm one of the highest paid and most requested speakers in tech in the United States. I would have never in a million years guessed that that would be the case way back when.

The speaking circuit is one of the best ways to monetize your expertise; not only can it be an extremely lucrative income stream, it can also be a great way to meet people in your ecosystem and spread the word about your company. Note that there are some times that you speak for free when representing your company. Each gig is a little different. Here are ten steps that can take you from never having spoken in front of an audience to being paid to speak, within six months:

1. **Get clear on your goals.** Consider the reason you want this additional income stream. Is it for a dream family vacation? Is it a way to boost your financial security? Is it to earn money that you will put aside to invest in three or four start-ups next year? Or is it to fund the cost of taking a course or attending a conference? It's important to know your "why" from the outset.

2. **Identify possible topics.** Make a list of five to ten topics that you could confidently talk about for twenty minutes uninterrupted. Each topic can be something you enjoy doing in your free time, the job or industry you're in, how you started a company, a hack that you're good at, traveling tips...anything you have some experience with. Online marketing expert Amy Porterfield says your expertise needs to be only 10% ahead of your audience's knowledge in order to be impactful and helpful to them. So don't think that unless you're a master at something you have nothing to share.

3. **Research.** Look up conferences that are happening six or more months out. Write down three that you'd love to join as a speaker.

4. **Practice.** In order to create a speaker reel, you'll need to get some speaking gigs booked. To begin with, you should offer to speak for free. Search online for conferences happening near you or virtually. If you're already going to a conference, contact the organizers and ask if you can get some time to speak for free. Even if it's just five minutes of stage time prior to someone else's presentation, it's still worth doing. You could contact your high school or your college and ask to speak there. Some companies have "lunch and learn" programs where an employee can give a talk. Check out your local community hubs, such as libraries and community colleges. As long as you have an audience, it's an event!

5. **Create your speaker reel.** Once you've had some practice, the next step is putting together your speaker reel. A speaker reel is usually between sixty seconds and three minutes long, and it highlights what someone is getting when they hire you as a speaker. You will need to have someone film the material for your speaker reel; this could be a trusted friend, or you could hire someone for an hour. Ensure that you not only get

some footage of you onstage but also of the audience looking interested. If you have access to a microphone, that's even better, as your reel will look and sound more professional. You will want to make the reel as dynamic as possible since this is your selling tool.

6. **Get testimonials.** Another important piece of content to get from these free speaking gigs is testimonials. If you can get someone from the audience or from the conference organization to give you a sentence or two about your performance, you can then add that to your reel or website.

7. **Set your fee.** Take your current yearly salary and divide it by thirty. This will determine what you can charge per speaking event, starting out. This is not based on any particular science, but it is the method I used when I first started. If you don't currently have any income, that's okay — start at $500 or $1,000. If I had tried to become a speaker when I was thirty years old, I would have been dividing zero by thirty! If the event involves travel, you may want to add that on to the cost as well; sometimes the organization will book travel for you, sometimes you will book it and be reimbursed, or sometimes they will just add an amount of money to your fee to cover any expenses. To begin with, you'll probably have to pay for your own travel, so try to keep your bookings local. Always find out

whether you will be reimbursed for travel before booking the gig. Don't forget that the figure you're charging is not merely for forty-five minutes of your time. You're charging for the years of experience you have, the knowledge that you amassed to get to this point. Be willing to say no to the wrong opportunities in order to get the right ones. Your rate will get higher over time with experience.

8. **Build a website.** There are so many tools that have made website design accessible so that anyone can have their own professional website without too much hassle. Place your speaker reel front and center. Include your contact information within the reel as well as on the website, in case someone sees the video on another site, such as YouTube or Vimeo. You want to ensure that people can always find you! Don't forget to include a short biography about yourself on your website. You will also want an intake form so that people can book you through the website. If you're interested in getting an agent, send the website link to ten or more speaking agencies. You can visit GravitySpeakers.com to see an example of a legit agency (mine). Acquiring an agent may take time; try to find some reviews of agencies, and make sure to do your research. Ask if they'll represent you, give them your rate, and note that they'll take anywhere from 15% to 30% of the fee. You will

THE IMPORTANCE OF OWNERSHIP

still need to be proactive in finding opportunities, but your speaking agent will help you negotiate and organize logistics. It's a partnership and has always been worth the fee in my experience.

9. **Return to your aspirational list of future conferences.** Your agent should reach out to them at least three months in advance (sometimes earlier) and present them with your website, speaker reel, and rate. If you don't have an agent, you can contact the conference organizations yourself with the same information. You will probably be turned down the first few times, even when you're offering to speak for free, and that's okay. Eventually you'll get a yes, which will lead to another yes, and eventually a lot more yeses. Once you've established a proven track record, if you receive pushback about your rate or the fact that you're charging at all, you're probably pursuing the wrong events. Some events can't afford to pay speakers, but if they have sponsors and are charging a ticket rate and they don't want to pay you for your time, they're not worth it. When you settle for less than you're worth, you bring everyone else down too because the organizers know they can hire you for cheaper. It's a no-win: you'll be undercutting other people and not respecting your own worth. That said, some events are worth doing for free because of all the great exposure and

networking you'll get out of them. In the case of annual summits hosted by established news outlets (Forbes, Fortune, etc., which usually do not pay) and huge events such as the South by Southwest (SXSW) festival, for example, the opportunity to speak in front of that many people is payment in itself.

10. **Enjoy yourself!** Enjoy the experience of sharing your expertise and the people it puts you in contact with. I know someone who had their company acquired by Amazon after someone high up saw them speaking at one event. I know others who have sold hundreds of books after speaking. I personally have made six-figure deals happen on the backs of speaking events. But none of that compares with the joy you'll get from people coming up to you to tell you how much your words have helped and inspired them. People still approach me to thank me for things I've said at a conference four years prior. If you can get yourself the platform to lift others up while earning money in the process, use it!

CHAPTER 12

DON'T COUNT ON THE MONEY UNTIL IT'S IN THE BANK

No matter how you decide to fund your business, don't forget that until the money is sitting in your company bank account, you cannot count on it. Never spend the money before you have it. There have been so many times when I've been certain that Backstage Capital was going to get funding from an investor or a firm, and it's fallen through at the last minute.

In 2018, Backstage Capital was on the brink of something big — and so was I. I'd been featured on the cover of

Fast Company magazine (the first noncelebrity Black woman to get the cover), we'd been investing in amazing founders with companies I was excited about, and I'd been the subject of the seventh season of the Gimlet podcast *StartUp*. Meanwhile, Backstage Capital was in talks with the venture arm of the Renault-Nissan-Mitsubishi Alliance, the world's leading automotive alliance. I'd met an executive of the fund in Nashville when we'd spoken on a panel together, and a few weeks later he saw my *Fast Company* cover at the airport and got in touch. We had weeks of conversations about what Alliance Ventures could do for Backstage, and eventually we met for an in-person meeting, with all of Backstage's top executives flying into San Francisco from different parts of the country. We met with three or four of their major executives and had a great conversation. The Alliance fund was going to invest $5 million into Backstage operations. This money would be used to cover our operating expenses (rather than used to invest in other companies), and it would fill the gap where the management fee would usually be.

We knew that having that kind of money behind us would completely change our world. It meant that our team would have a financial runway for years. The Alliance executives also let us know that this would be just the beginning of a decade-long relationship. They weren't looking to turn a quick profit and bolt; their aim was to invest long-term. There were actual tears shed on both sides of the table because we were all so excited about this partnership and all felt so aligned in our mission and our work. It was such an exciting moment, especially after several years of financing our operations on $25,000 checks at a time. Five million dollars was going to change everything! I was on cloud nine.

Although we had a verbal agreement, we hadn't yet signed anything. The plan was to meet the president of Alliance, Carlos Ghosn, who would sign the papers and smile for the camera, and then we would be ready to go with $5 million in our account. Carlos was always traveling, so we scheduled the meeting for a few weeks later, at a time he would already be in the country.

Fast-forward two weeks: I'm waking up in a hotel in New York City, sitting in bed and looking at my Twitter feed. As I scan the trending news, I have to blink my eyes a couple of times to make sure I'm seeing and reading what I think I am. Two weeks after meeting the Alliance team, the third-highest trending topic in the world is Carlos Ghosn. It's because he's been arrested.

The guy who was going to put his signature on a piece of paper that said Backstage had a $5 million deal with his company had been arrested for all kinds of white-collar crimes, including misusing company funds. I felt like I was out of body, like I was in shock. For a moment there was silence and then I actually started laughing, chuckling to myself and thinking, *Of course. Of course this would happen. Not only would the deal fall through but it would fall through like this, in a global, public way, like in a $100 million movie that Michael Bay or Aaron Sorkin might develop.* Then my heart sank and I was devastated, wondering, *Well, what do we do now? Where do we go from here?*

As soon as I could, I got on the phone with the executive from Alliance that I had been working with. He was despondent. I think he was in shock too. So I said to him, "Hey, so we're still on, right?" I was half joking but half hoping that somehow this didn't affect us. He said to me, "I don't know what to tell you. I know exactly what you know, and I have a lot of things I have to think about today." I knew he had much bigger problems on his hands than I did at that moment, so I left it at that. But that was the last time we ever spoke. We never got our $5 million, and we never heard from Alliance again.

It was frustrating to be so close to a deal like that and have it slip through our fingers, because we really needed it at that moment. Unfortunately, it wouldn't be the last time something like that happened. But it reminded me to have thick skin and to not put all my eggs in one basket. There's only so much time you can spend mourning a loss like that, because your company and your employees need you to figure out a way to keep going. Now, when I meet with investors, I go into things expecting nothing, because nothing is real until the money is in the bank. It'll save you a lot of time and heartache if you know that from the beginning; it gives you that inner strength that will sustain you through the tough times. In business as in life, the best way around disappointment is through it.

Carlos Ghosn's story didn't end with his arrest. After being held in Japan under custody and house arrest for a year, he escaped Japan in a shipping container in December of 2019 and flew to Lebanon. As of this writing, he is still living in exile in Beirut.

Exercises

It's life audit time! Make a list of your desires, hopes, aspirations. Make a second list of your resources. Finally, connect the two and look for what you're missing. What resources are you missing that will get you closer to the life you want? Where can you find those resources? What changes can you make to move closer to your aspirations?

PART THREE

MANY MINI EMPIRES

In my first book, *It's About Damn Time*, I explained that no one in this world is "self-made." No business executive, no artist, no inventor, no one. It's not possible to do everything yourself, and it's not possible to be untouched by the helping hands around you — however faint they feel. To say you are self-made is to encourage the myth of the lone genius who claims they got to where they are because they worked harder than anyone else. But this view ignores the role of privilege, both systemic and acquired, and understates the importance, the power, and the beauty of collaboration. **Collaboration isn't just important — it's actually a hack, and one I've used throughout my career.** In every situation there is a way to make things easier through collaboration. So why make things harder for yourself? There's no medal for doing things the hard way, and when you collaborate with others, you increase your value *and* theirs. You can hack your way into a wider audience, a more innovative technology, and/or larger-scale social change, all by working with others.

We should be proud to have worked with other people, to have helped others out and to have received that help ourselves. We all know that we're stronger together, so why do we keep emphasizing this lone wolf ideal in the world of business? None of this has to be a race to the top; there absolutely can be more than just one winner. We need to help one another climb higher and create winners everywhere.

CHAPTER 13

CREATING WINNERS EVERYWHERE

I'm often asked in interviews, "What do you see the world looking like in the next five or ten years?" When I imagine the future, I see a lot of currently underestimated people doing really well. I see them building mini empires in different cities, working on improving life for the people in their community.

It's already evident that in the future, we won't be flying out to Silicon Valley for all our big meetings — the use of technology during the coronavirus pandemic has shown that this isn't necessary. We no longer need to think of Silicon Valley as the home of all start-ups; we no longer have to add the cost of a plane ticket and a hotel stay to the tight budget of an entrepreneur. But this isn't just because we're taking meetings through Zoom; it's because that location no longer has to have such a hold over people. This means more equal opportunities. What if the best person for the job lives on the other side of the country? Or even in another country? We're seeing it already in hubs around the United States — cities that have started their own local ecosystems and created opportunities for the people that live there. Not only does this create more opportunities for underestimated founders, it could also lead to a better quality of life for those founders who are no longer forced to live in or commute to a region that is both extremely expensive and racially homogenous. When the old boys' club won't let you in, it only makes sense to start your own club.

When my venture firm announced our Backstage Accelerator program in 2018, we knew how important it would be to place the accelerators in different cities. The first three cities were Los Angeles, Philadelphia, and London. We let the public vote for the fourth city, and Detroit won. We were thrilled with this result. Internally we had a list of the cities where we knew we had contacts and resources, and we thought it was likely that NYC or Atlanta would win because there were a lot of people already building these hubs. When Detroit won, it showed us that our community was excited about a popular vote, and it was cool to see that a city like Detroit, which had been long abandoned by the coastal elite, could go toe-to-toe with hubs like NYC and Atlanta and actually win. The fact that thousands of people took part in the vote and wanted their city to win just goes to show how many aspiring entrepreneurs there are all over the United States (and the rest of the world). Geographic disparity is just another way in which underestimated people are kept out of the venture capital world. If you don't have the means to fly out to the West Coast, or your business idea is something that is hard to understand without the knowledge of your local area, you're left out. I want to see an equality of opportunity.

This is why I am committed to creating one thousand millionaires instead of the next lone billionaire. I want a future where we can't name ten billionaires who have more wealth combined than the rest of the world. Where what we buy and where we work doesn't depend on the whims of extremely rich men who all live in the same place and come from the same background. It's an actual vision I see, and I want you to imagine it too. **What would it look like if the wealthiest people in the country were actually representative of the population of the United States?**

I find it interesting to imagine what it would look like and what it would mean for the next decade or generation if the richest people in America lived in different parts of the country, had different life experiences, and came from different cultures. What could it mean for policy, for health care, for who is in office, for whether the potholes on your street get fixed, if there were a thousand millionaires who had a diverse range of experiences of school, work, and different cultures? I'd like to see more marginalized people wielding power and having a say in what happens in their neighborhoods and their communities. On my podcast *Your First Million* (episode 31), musician Yello-Pain spoke about how we can empower ourselves and our communities by voting. Like many people in the United States, he used to believe that his vote didn't count and that there was no point in voting. When he learned more about it, he realized that the people in power *wanted* people like him to feel that way. He made it his mission to educate citizens about the importance of voting, explaining that the people who vote the most have the most. Three years later, YelloPain independently produced a brilliant movie called *Simplified: Bridging the Gap,* which helps educators to explain complex voting issues to young people from minority backgrounds.

I want to look around and see so many more of us in the rooms where decisions get made. Once we're there, it's up to us to be the people we wished those in power would have been all this time, to be the ones using our wealth in a way that helps others and creates a better quality of life for everyone. To me, that's so much more interesting than being another venture capitalist who gets rich from investing in a unicorn company — why it has been more interesting for us at Backstage to have 6,500 people (at the time of writing) each investing to a total of $5 million in our management entity via Reg CF (Regulation Crowdfunding) rather than one person investing $5 million. Any day of the week, that's going to be more exciting, more interesting, to me. Most investors don't feel that way, because opening up their equity to crowdfunding involves a lot of transparency or because they might feel like they have to give up too much of their own equity.

I'm going to say it loudly for those at the back: I'm giving out the gold coins because I think there is a better quality of life if we all get a piece of the pie. As my net worth grows, you will see me take substantial amounts of my wealth and distribute it. Because this is what I really believe — it's not something I'm just saying. When you give back, you create a network and a community, two of the most powerful tools you can have in your toolbox.

Collaboration doesn't necessarily have to happen in person. What the pandemic has proven is that working remotely is absolutely possible, and more effective than it was previously thought; in fact, Backstage Capital has always been staffed by a remote team, so when the pandemic hit, we didn't have to think about getting out of an office lease or getting laptops sent out to staff, because we were already working from our homes. Remote work is great for a number of reasons, the main being that location no longer has to dictate jobs and priorities. Why have one large hub for venture capital and innovation when you could have many small communities all over the country (and all over the world)?

CHAPTER 14

CHOOSING YOUR COLLABORATORS CAREFULLY

Collaboration can be a beautiful way to share your success with others (and vice versa), but it's not always easy to know who to collaborate with. Not all partners in business are going to be equal, and deciding who you work with and who you associate with publicly can make or break your business. In other words, choosing your collaborators carefully is very important. You need to know going into the collaboration what it is that you both want to get out of it, and you need to make sure that those expectations are clearly spelled out.

When a collaboration is unequal, it can become less of a partnership. In start-up culture, it can be difficult not to be persuaded by a large check when that's what you need to get your company started, but not all money is equal, either. When I was first starting Backstage Capital, I linked up with two investors who had been successful funders in Europe. At the time, I felt like this was the best way to get into the world of venture capital. I needed a Trojan horse, someone to walk me into rooms I couldn't get into and give me the kudos that comes with having the "right connections." Over email, these two men understood what I was talking about, they liked my idea, and it was going to be cool. We were going to share all the financial economics. I took our first meeting over the phone in a rental car. I was still sharing a hotel room with my mom at this point, relying on food stamps for my groceries. I had no money, and I really believed that this would be the best way to get started doing what I knew I could do. I was the one who had introduced these two men to each other and thought I was creating a match that would be good for all three of us. But minutes into the very first phone call, I knew it wasn't going to work. They completely bulldozed me. They talked over me, and they didn't take anything I said at face value. After the meeting, I wrote to them and let them know that as much as I would have loved it to work, it wasn't going to. I turned down a lot of capital at a point when I barely had enough money to live, never mind get my business off the ground.

It can be tempting in circumstances like these to just take the money when it's offered. But collaboration is about equality, respect, and understanding your role, and with these two men, it would not have been a collaboration. The fact that I needed the money so badly — and that those men knew it — created a major power imbalance, and I had too much respect for myself — and for my vision — to allow my dream to be diluted by that. Power dynamics exist in every collaboration, and it's important to be aware of what those are, especially when money is involved.

CHAPTER 15

MATCHMAKING

Natasha Case is the cofounder of Coolhaus, an innovative ice cream company that Backstage Capital proudly invested in and that has grown exponentially since starting back in 2009. When interviewed on my podcast (episode 65), Natasha explained that one of the best ways to grow an audience is by creating unexpected partnerships. Rather than partnering with something obvious, like a chocolate or candy company, Coolhaus has collaborated with brands such as French's Mustard and Ritz Crackers, which are certainly not the first things that come to mind when you think of ice cream. That was exactly the point: with each partner, a product was created that intrigued people and got them talking. Natasha explained, "It's this really special, surprise experience. It's really different. We talk about it on all our channels. We send it to press and bloggers. For example, with the French's Mustard one, this mustard ice cream that was strangely addictive, even though it sounds disgusting..."[*]

But the benefits of these partnerships went beyond just word of mouth. The thing is, Natasha told me, French's is owned by McCormick & Company, the largest producer of spices and related products. With more than thirty brands under their umbrella, McCormick had some of the biggest PR and marketing agencies at their disposal, she said. "They have the budget to help us give it out and reach people. We have the speed to market, we have the unique channel with the trucks, we have the cool factor. You get this huge win-win, and it just becomes this storm of excitement around ice cream....It's marketing that pays for itself, plus some. We're getting paid to do what we do best, but we're growing our brand awareness."

When I asked her what type of partnerships she looks for, Natasha replied that the best partners are the ones that complement and elevate each other; she cautioned

---

[*] Arlan Hamilton and Natasha Case, "Coolhaus Ice Cream Founder Natasha Case on Delivering Deliciousness," April 1, 2021, in *Your First Million*, produced by Anna Eichenauer and Bryan Landers, podcast, https://podcasts.apple.com/us/podcast/your-first-million/id1467515562?i=1000515330645.

against partnering with people or companies that are doing the same kind of thing as you, because that can mean that you already have the same audience so the opportunity for growth isn't as big. When you find a person or company that complements your brand but has a different kind of reach and audience, you each get to be seen by a whole new set of potential customers. It also helps if you each have different strengths when it comes to marketing and promotion; for example, maybe you have a large TikTok following, and your partner puts on great live events. The goal is to find partners who align with your ideals but are different enough to create audience growth.

In 2022, Coolhaus was acquired by The Urgent Company, a sustainable food brand. When deciding whether to accept the deal offered by The Urgent Company, Natasha considered what Coolhaus needed and what the company could offer them. As they had very similar missions but very different resources, this collaboration made total sense. Natasha described it in a Medium post as "a win/win for both companies," noting that they could "empower one another to achieve our goals."[*]

Collaboration isn't always about an exchange between

---

[*] Megan Rose Dickey, "Coolhaus Acquisition Marks One of Backstage Capital's First 'True Exits,'" Medium (website), January 24, 2022, https://medium.com/greenroom/coolhaus-acquisition-marks-one-of-backstage-capitals-first-true-exits-a5bed2baedb8.

two parties. Collaboration builds networks, and networks are hugely important and helpful in both the world of work and in your personal life. Sometimes collaboration is helping out others by introducing them to someone who can help them. This matchmaking has played a huge role in my career.

I've always been interested in people. This curiosity is a big part of what has propelled me forward at every point in my life. For instance, when I was twenty-two, I set a challenge for myself to meet ten thousand people, thinking that I would complete the challenge in a matter of months. But every time I met someone new, I was so interested in their story that the meeting ended up taking much longer than I had predicted. On the very first day I started the challenge, I met two women (separately) who didn't know each other but lived in the same city and had a niche interest in common. One was a young woman who wanted to work with orangutans, and the other was an older woman who already did work with orangutans. It blew my mind at the time — I couldn't believe I was meeting these two women within hours of each other. But I didn't have a way to connect the two of them, and I've always wondered what would have happened if I'd been able to introduce them that night.

I love to matchmake, and I have always been pretty good at it. That goes for business too. When I started researching and learning about funding disparities in the venture capital world, those matchmaking instincts ended up coming in handy. I was completely broke at the time but figured that what I lacked in physical capital, I would have to make up for in social capital. I'd always been drawn to entrepreneurs, so I already had some in my network, but the more I learned about start-ups and venture funds, and the more I engaged in online conversations on the topic of funding disparities, the more new people I interacted with and added to my network. Pretty soon I started connecting people in my network with one another; if I met someone with a problem that I knew someone else in my network could help solve, I was able to be the person who connected them. By doing this I created a community of underestimated founders who could pool their knowledge and resources about different investors and help one another out.

CHAPTER 16

BUILDING YOUR TEAM

I first had the idea for my company Runner in 2017. At the time, I was building Backstage Capital, and I knew I didn't have the capacity to work on both ideas at once. I decided I had to build Backstage Capital first because I needed to become the venture capitalist I was looking for as a founder. I also wanted to build the kind of workplace where I'd want to work, where even once you'd moved on to other things, you were still considered part of the community, an alumnus of the company. Once I did that, I had a little more space to consider how to be the founder I'd look for as a venture capitalist. I've been working since I was fifteen years old, and I've always wanted to become the boss that I would have liked to work for.

I started Runner, a company that helps connect part-time and temporary operations and HR talent with inclusive companies, because I understand how important these operations jobs are and how much companies rely on these employees. As someone who did gig work for many years prior to entering the venture capital industry, I also wanted to find a way to make temporary work better for the employee: something that was more reliable, that included some kind of benefits, and that was flexible in a way that benefited both the employer and the employee. When I was getting Backstage off the ground, I had to hire people on a temporary, part-time basis because I couldn't yet afford to pay someone for more than a few hours a week. Finding someone who could do high-level work but on a flexible, part-time schedule was really difficult, so I mostly reached out to people through my social circle. That's how I found my executive assistant and other key members of my team. As my business grew, I was able to employ them on a full-time, long-term basis.

What I liked about gig work was that you didn't necessarily have to work the corporate nine-to-five. I wanted to create a service that helped talented people find that kind of gig work while also helping companies find talented people. If Runner had existed several years before, I would have signed up to be a "runner" in a heartbeat. I am certain I wouldn't have been homeless or on food stamps as a result. This insight was my North Star in launching the company.

Runner is all about matchmaking. We match runners — individuals who are looking for work, who tell us about their skills and experience and what kind of work they want to do — with our customers — founders, large corporations, and the like, who tell us what they're looking for. But to find the best fit for both sides of the equation, we look at more than just skills and experience; we match people by understanding their core values and whether they align with a company's mission. If you as an employer can hire someone for a job that aligns with their values and their passion, you are going to get a better worker and will be able to keep that person for much longer. I always tell people to **"be yourself so the people looking for you can find you,"** and I live by that. When you mix someone like me, who is so naturally curious, with people who are truly themselves — honest and open and who bring their whole self to everything they do — amazing opportunities arise. Remember, every person has something that they are expert in. If you can match those people up with those who need their expertise, magic happens.

You don't need to start a company to do this. All you need is creativity and the ability to observe and listen. In a

2021 interview, Oprah Winfrey asked Eddie Murphy how he got to be such a great comedian, and he said he thinks the greatest comedians are the ones who observe everything in the room. They're the ones who notice even the smallest, seemingly insignificant details and are able to connect the dots very quickly. That's what you need to do in order to connect people in a thoughtful way.

CHAPTER 17

YOUR NETWORK IS CURRENCY

Having a wide network is one of the best ways to increase your value — but not for the reasons people typically think. Every new connection you make increases the number of people you can connect with one another. When you connect two people, you're showing both of them the value you have: the ability to connect them to the things and people they want and need.

When people ask me how to get into tech, I tell them the best thing they can do is start clicking around on socials, reading, following others, and creating networks. If you have the curiosity required, you'll make valuable connections in no time, without even leaving the house. Community is all about the connections, the ties, the shared experiences, and the shared knowledge.

Unfortunately, networks have historically been systems that have kept underestimated founders out of the club. Social media and online conferences have changed this to a certain extent; there is no limit to how many people you can get to know online, and there is only so much a conference organizer can charge for a ticket to a live stream event. Your network can be valuable in so many different ways, and that doesn't always have to mean connecting with the wealthy or powerful.

Today, the power of your network lies not only in quality and quantity but also in **diversity.** It's worth more to connect with someone who shares your ideas than with someone who is wealthy or powerful but whose ideals don't align with your own. It's worth more to connect with five different people with different backgrounds, experiences, and expertise than with fifty people with virtually identical backgrounds, experiences, and expertise. When you are part of a diverse network, you have the chance to connect with people who can widen your worldview. Plus, you are far more likely to create products and services that appeal to a wide range of people if your network is diverse.

Never stop learning when it comes to your network; let your curiosity lead you to people and places unknown.

It can be more valuable — and much easier — to network horizontally, with people at similar stages of business, than to network vertically, with people who are multiple steps ahead of you. On *Your First Million* (bonus episode released in September of 2020), when I asked Mark Cuban, a billionaire, why he invested $6 million into my fund when he doesn't usually enjoy investing in other people's funds, he said without hesitation, "You're in rooms I'll never be in."[*] Think about how powerful that is. Mark Cuban is worth five to six billion dollars at any given time — multiples of what I'm worth today. That'll change, but in the meantime, he still comes to ask me questions. When Mark was asked in 2020 whom he looks to for investing advice, he said, "Warren Buffett, Ray Dalio, and Arlan Hamilton." Think about how much *your* network could be worth. You don't have to be rich to be powerful.

Think about building your network and building your reputation as one and the same. When I say "reputation," I don't mean your personal branding. A brand is what you put out into the world; it's the way you *want* people to see you, and you can have a lot of control over what that looks like. **Reputation is your brand in real time.** It's what people

---

[*] Arlan Hamilton and Mark Cuban, "My $6M Fund with Mark Cuban," September 25, 2020, in *Your First Million*, produced by Anna Eichenauer and Bryan Landers, podcast, https://podcasts.apple.com/us/podcast/your-first-million/id1467515562?i=1000492555130.

think of when they hear your name, the things people will say about you when you're not around. It's important! How you treat others will always reflect on you and, in turn, people's desire to connect with you. Your network is built over decades. Look ahead at preserving relationships for the long haul. Don't burn your bridges because someone is on a different timeline than you. If you connect with someone, don't expect to get something out of them immediately. Your network is about knowledge and connection, not transaction. You can never know what another person might accomplish or how they might be helpful to you in the future — and vice versa. No one is too small or unimportant for your network.

With the help of technology, we can be part of many communities at once. Being a part of multiple communities allows us to be our full, authentic selves; we don't need to try to fit into someone else's mold. If the community we want to join doesn't exist, we can simply build our own. Why waste time trying to get into someone else's empire? Why shrink yourself to suit someone else's vision? Build your own empire and make your own rules.

What stops me from worrying about being hungry or homeless again is not my wealth, it's my network. It's like a shield around me. In exchange, I'm proud to be a part of so many other shields as well.

CHAPTER 18

GETTING INTO THE ROOM

When building your network, sometimes what you need is the opportunity to get into the right room with the right people. So what do you do if you're struggling to get into those rooms? If you're broke and can't afford a conference ticket? If you don't have anyone to introduce you to the person? A few years ago, back when I still worked in the music industry, I was between jobs and totally broke. I was sleeping on a friend's couch in LA, and I'd just been through a really bad breakup. Things felt really rough. I badly needed to get a new gig on the road but I didn't have any leads. I found out about a convention happening in Arizona; I couldn't afford a ticket to the convention, and I couldn't afford a plane ticket, but I bought a $15 ticket for a bus that would take me to Arizona overnight. I arrived with a stiff neck, no money, nowhere to sleep beyond the first night, and still no ticket, just hoping I could make it work. I knew I had to get into that convention, so I arrived at the venue just as they opened and asked one of the organizers if I could volunteer at the front desk in exchange for being allowed into a couple of the lectures or panels during a break. They agreed, and I spent the next three days sitting at the front desk handing out name tags and answering questions. I started meeting people straightaway because I was the first person they saw when they arrived; I used my charm and information I knew from research — as I said in my first book, *be the money* — and told them a little bit about my story so far and my experience in the industry. Those conversations turned out to be more valuable than the lectures themselves. Three days later, I had a gig working with Toni Braxton after meeting her production manager and striking up a conversation. I had arrived with literally nothing and left with an opportunity!

I recently went to see a show at the Comedy Store, a comedy club in West Hollywood, and witnessed a similar hack. I was shown to my seat by a Black woman who worked at the venue, and ten minutes later, she was up onstage. She had obviously asked for five minutes of stage time, and as a result, she was getting to practice her comedy material on a real audience, at a real comedy club; she got to open for the opener. This is the kind of thing that can unlock so many doors for you; **if you can use your ingenuity to get into that room with the right people, you're on your way.** You have to take opportunities when they arise, but even more important is that you create opportunities when they don't. If you want to break into a new industry but lack the experience, can you be an intern or volunteer? If you want to be on that stage, can you work the door or take people to their seats? If you want to get into a fancy party or event with lots of movers and shakers, can you volunteer to check coats? Make a list of the conferences, events, or networking opportunities you want to attend over the next three, four, or five months and figure out an ethical, clever way in.

Dawn Dickson is the queen of networking. A serial entrepreneur, she has founded five companies, and she's a keynote speaker, an inventor, and a trailblazer in the crowdfunding space. In 2019, she became the first Black woman to raise one million dollars through equity crowdfunding. She was able to do that because she understands the absolute importance of networking horizontally — that is, networking with the people around you. When I interviewed her for my podcast (episode 6) in 2019, she described networking as "building mutually beneficial relationships that span time."* She explained that before Backstage Capital invested in her software company PopCom, she spent eight months "following up and showing up and supporting and retweeting and not just showing that I just want something from you, but that I can extend whatever I have to offer."

Dawn understands the value of the smallest things, noting that if someone can't afford to invest, even a retweet of her campaign is valuable. For this reason, she believes that everyone has something they can bring to the table. Having been in the tech industry for a long time, she has built a network that is spread far and wide. She noted on my podcast, "I've been an entrepreneur nineteen years and I've been building relationships for that long and being a person of integrity, being out there, having my face in the room." This goes back to the importance of reputation. If you work with integrity like Dawn, and you honor your networks, it's likely your reputation will be positive. "Before I was on the stages," she said, "I was in the seats. Before

---

* Arlan Hamilton and Dawn Dickson, "I Bridge the Gap Between Venture Capital and Everyday People," June 29, 2019, in *Your First Million*, produced by Anna Eichenauer and Bryan Landers, podcast, https://podcasts.apple.com/us/podcast/your-first-million/id1467515562?i=1000443151974.

they were having me come to speak, I was in line to talk to the speakers...." Dawn paid to be in those seats because she understood that showing up mattered and because she understood that going to conferences was an investment in herself and in building her network — that even just a casual conversation with the person sitting next to her could lead to valuable gains in the future. "And I was always very deliberate and intentional with my networking, and what I wanted to gain, and what I had to offer," she explained.

When it came time to raise money for PopCom, the network she had created gave her options. So when most venture capitalists weren't interested in her company, she realized she was talking to the wrong people and started pitching to her community instead. She wasn't getting the respect she deserved in venture, so she stopped knocking on the doors that no one would answer and instead turned to her network. Dawn believed that "you can source everything from your own community. Everything you want to get, you can get from your tribe." And she was right. Her tribe was how she got onto The Breakfast Club and Shade Room, online platforms where she could speak directly to her community and offer them the opportunity of owning a piece of her company through equity crowdfunding. For her, raising funds this way meant that she had the opportunity to create wealth not only for herself and her team members but also for her community. When she looks into the future, she said, "I can see 2,300 people getting money out of this."*

Dawn's story highlights the fact that networking and community building are long-term affairs. Time can be an investment that brings high ROI, which is why you never really finish building and nurturing your network. Through equity crowdfunding, Dawn also built a new community of investors with their own networks. When organizing meet and greets, she told attendees, "Don't come to meet-and-greet me. I'm putting you in the room with one hundred other investors in your city." By investing in her company, they too had gained access to a network of other investors. She noted, "Horizontal networking increases vertical advancement. We build up together." She proved this a year later when she raised another million dollars through equity crowdfunding, despite the added challenge of an ongoing pandemic.

---

* Legal notice: This is not a guarantee, as all start-up investing is inherently risky. Please always conduct due diligence before investing.

CHAPTER 19

CALLING ON EXPERTS

Arlan's Academy began as one course, which I created in April of 2020. It was a reaction to the COVID pandemic and being stuck at home for the first time in three years. I'm always looking for new ways to share knowledge and catalyze others. I know from the number of emails I get — and questions in interviews, and direct messages on social media — that I have information that is worth sharing. I know I'm an expert in raising start-up capital, as I've been raising and investing for years now. So I created a course to teach others what I've spent years learning.

The moment things really changed, though, was when I

chose to reach out to other people and collaborate. I knew other experts could do the same thing—share their knowledge and expertise, make money during this difficult time—and by reaching out to others, I could create a teaching platform that could be really useful. None of us are experts in everything, and if you want to create a valuable resource, you need to find people who will share the expertise that you don't have. That's how what started as just a single course has become a platform with almost thirty tutors teaching all kinds of different skill sets, and every one of them is an expert in their field—as a bonus, most are women of color. Lawyers, doctors, professors, founders, executives, all with their expertise.

Everyone has something they can teach to others. If you're having trouble figuring out what that topic is for you, think of something you do for your career or hobby at least once per week and deconstruct how you do it, even down to the smallest, most obvious detail. That's your first one-hour course. Then find someone with expertise that complements yours and explore how you might work together. My *Your First Million* episodes with Amy Porterfield (episode 91) and Danielle Leslie (episode 98) will teach you how to turn those collaborations into meaningful income.

Exercises

+ Social media can be a great way to meet new people that are outside of your usual social circle. Some of my best hires for Backstage Capital were people I met on Twitter who showed an interest in what I was doing. Reach out to ten new people on social media and see where those relationships take you.

+ Don't be shy about reaching out to people whose North Star aligns with yours, even if they feel "out of your league." They may have hundreds of thousands of social media followers, a fancy job title, or a successful company, but that doesn't mean you have nothing to offer them. If you move in different circles, you may have more to offer! Make a list of five people with whom your North Star aligns and send them a message.

+ Attending conferences can be another great way to meet people; if you can't afford a ticket to a conference, ask whether they need volunteers. You'll get access to all the attendees, and you'll also get to know the organizers, which might be even more fruitful. Make a list of three conferences you would like to attend this year, and then start looking into how you can make that happen.

PART FOUR

REDEFINING SUCCESS

L ately, I've been asked a lot about what the future of work looks like. It's a question on many people's minds because, for a large percentage of the world, work changed in 2020. For some, work became more dangerous, more of a personal risk with every shift at the grocery store. Some experienced a new loneliness, working from home, while others discovered the joys of no longer commuting, a flexible schedule, and working from the comfort of a home office. Parents worked double or triple shifts, doing Zoom calls while supervising their children's schooling, trying to be teacher, parent, and employee or employer all at once. Some small business owners spent hours or days without a single customer walking through their doors, while others were forced to close their doors altogether. Hospital workers were pushed to the absolute brink of desperation, risking their lives every day and losing patients in numbers never seen before. They covered extra shifts, found work-arounds to ensure that essential services could be carried out while also protecting their staff, and dealt with the inevitable spread of COVID-19 as well as the mental toll of the tragedy and grief they encountered daily. No person's work was unaffected. So it makes sense that the future of work feels less certain and less knowable. At the same time, when our idea of "normal" changes, we have the opportunity to use that momentum to create a *better* normal.

One of the clear lessons learned from the pandemic is that while we were all going through it together, each person's experience was actually very different. Working from home feels very different depending on what "home" is like for you — whether you have space for a desk, whether you live with other people, whether you have fast and reliable internet access. Working in a hospital or any other people-facing environment came with different risks for people who lived with or were caregivers to vulnerable loved ones. Our experience of work is circumstantial — it's contextual. While those in more privileged positions may not have realized it before the pandemic, it always has been this way, and it's about time we talked about that. One size has never, ever fit all. This is exactly what makes me excited about the future of work that we could have: a future where each person can curate a career that works with every part of their life...a future where employees have more power.

Executives love to talk about disruption, often as a justification for layoffs, pay cuts, or more hours spent at the office. But if anything needs "disrupting," it's the traditional power structures that govern the world of work. More and more, employers are finally being exposed for creating toxic workplaces. Companies that have long avoided unionization in their workforce are starting to see that brick wall crack, with the first unions being set up within Google, Amazon, and Starbucks. Slowly, the business world is learning that good employees are what make a business great, and no matter how charismatic the CEO is, they're useless without staff. No company works without employees. That is a power advantage, and we should be leveraging it.

For many companies, the Great Resignation resulting from the pandemic was a stark reminder that retaining employees is incredibly important, both organizationally and fiscally. Retaining employees requires treating them well, offering them opportunities for advancement, and ensuring they're able to get the benefits they need, such as health insurance and a retirement plan. This is why I am optimistic about the future of work as one that recognizes the humanity, individuality, and dignity of every worker.

If the future of work is one in which each individual has more power, more autonomy, and more choice, we must also consider how to make choices that align with our own individual definition of "success." Success is a malleable, ever-changing idea. It looks different to everyone, and yet it is often the people in power who get to define it for society. **When our success is defined by other people, we are likely to strive toward other people's goals.** What this means for underestimated people in particular is that the goalposts are often moved for us.

Some people equate success with hard work, and everyone loves a good rags-to-riches tale. Having grown up poor, I know for a fact that, as with most feel-good tales, the reality is a lot more complicated. I saw my mom work hard every day of my childhood, but we still struggled to get by on her salary. Some people are born into wealth and some people gain wealth through their occupation, but the salary you are paid does not always equate to the effort you put in. It may be that the job that you love, the thing that you've always wanted to do, just doesn't pay very well. But that doesn't mean you're going to work any less hard than you would if it did. Some of the most important jobs in the world are low-paying, which is a larger problem that needs to be solved. It is also proof that you don't have to be wealthy to be successful.

The first step toward being truly successful is knowing what that means for you. You can't follow a map to nowhere; you have to know what your destination is. Consider what you would like your life to look like — what is important to you, what is negotiable, and what is nonnegotiable. Look at your budget — how much money would you need to earn each month to consider yourself successful? Once you know that number, you can begin working toward it. This doesn't have to be a one-time decision, either. Your priorities and circumstances can change over the years, and your definition of success may be very different at a later point in life. Whatever that looks like, the important thing is that *you* get to decide.

CHAPTER 20

CHASING IMPACT, NOT UNICORNS

Everybody wants to feel successful and to be seen as successful. What that looks like has changed over time, depending on trends and how they are exhibited through popular culture. Sometimes that has meant expensive jewelry, cars, and yachts. Sometimes it has meant access to exclusive places or parties. Sometimes — including this current moment — it has meant having a degree from the right school, expressing the right political opinions, and consuming the right TV shows, newspapers, and books. But flaunting outward symbols of our perceived status is not the same as achieving true success.

We're a society taunted by comparisons; we follow influencers on social media, looking on enviously as they post photos of dining at cafés in Paris, lounging on white sand beaches, and opening packages of expensive gifts. If they're doing their job well, we can't help but yearn for that kind of lifestyle. The problem is that when we measure our success in comparisons, we are always going to lose out. If success is being the *most* rich, being the *most* powerful, having the *most* followers, then at this point, none of us are successful until we can build our own rocket and go to space. We could have all the money in the world, and there will always be people taking more luxurious vacations and buying bigger yachts. Does that mean we aren't successful? Hell no! We have to remember that *being* successful is *not* the same as *seeming* successful, even if our Instagram feed might make it appear otherwise.

It's time we start asking ourselves how *we* measure success. Is success a number in our bank account? A job title? How much revenue our business brings in, or how many customers it has? Or is success an action? **Personally, I measure success in impact, in change, in legacy.** Of course, this is not to say that you shouldn't aim to be wealthy — quite the opposite. But success doesn't start or end at one million dollars. **Money is the tool; success is the action it enables.**

In Silicon Valley, achieving "unicorn" status is considered

the ultimate marker of success for a company. A unicorn is a public company that is worth upwards of one billion dollars (on paper, at least); examples include Airbnb, Stripe, and Reddit. There's no denying that unicorns are successful by most conventional metrics, but do we have to look at success through such a narrow lens? There are companies that have made millions of dollars, have a huge loyal customer base, and are growing at a healthy rate, and yet, if they haven't hit the (often unrealistic) number investors set out for them, or they go public at only *half* a billion dollars, they're deemed failures. Does that sound like a failure to you? If your business is creating revenue that you can use to pay your rent, give your employees raises, and stay in the black, that is absolutely a success. If you have customers who love your product and recommend it to others, that is a success. We must stop thinking of success as a goalpost only the rarefied few will even reach, or we'll miss out on celebrating our achievements.

For example, my podcast *Your First Million* is something that I'm really proud of. I love choosing interesting guests, I love interviewing those guests, and I think it's a great resource for listeners. It's not the number one podcast on Apple or Spotify charts — it's not even in the top ten — and yet, statistically, every minute of every day, someone is listening to *Your First Million*. Hundreds of those listeners have posted reviews or written me emails telling me how much the podcast has inspired them. What if I had told myself, *Success is featuring in the top ten on podcast charts* or *Success is having five million listeners,* and *If I don't achieve that, I'm wasting my time?* I would never have gotten to experience the joy of making the episodes I have made and reaching the listeners I do have. So many opportunities have opened up to me because of *Your First Million* — opportunities I would have missed if I had measured my own success by someone else's definition and given up.

CHAPTER 21

DITCH THE FOMO

Success isn't about what your life looks like in an Instagram photo. It's about putting the power back in our hands. I believe the way we get to this point is to stop comparing ourselves. Instead of aspiring to be the wealthiest person, what if we could aspire to earn a six- or seven-figure income consistently year after year after year, doing something we enjoy, that we're good at, that fuels us and feeds our soul? Something that impacts others positively and leaves a legacy for us and our family?

Which brings me to the second step toward defining success on your own terms: ditch the FOMO (fear of missing out). FOMO can be a useful sales tactic if you're the one employing it. But it can also be used as a dangerous weapon. I used to suffer from FOMO, so I definitely know what it feels like, but I don't have it anymore. What this means for me is that I don't aspire to be any other person — not Oprah, Beyoncé, Shonda, Serena, Issa, or Ava. I can be impressed by them, moved by them, inspired by them, but I don't want what they have, I don't envy them, and I don't want to *be* them. I want to be Arlan — that's my goal.

And by the same token, I don't want *you* to want to be me; hopefully you'll be inspired by me, and you'll learn from me, but as just one lesson among many others you'll pick up in the academy of life.

Not having FOMO has kept me focused, because I no longer get distracted by what other people are doing. Back in 2017, I had a little notoriety in the tech space, and there were a couple of big magazine covers out there that featured groups of game-changing female investors. At the time, several people said to me, "They should have had you there — aren't you upset?" But I wasn't — I was just happy for those women. I bought the magazines, read them, and celebrated them. I knew my time would come and I would get what I deserved at the right time. In 2018, I was asked to be on the cover of *Fast Company* magazine in the United States and South Africa. That cover story changed my life. Can you imagine if I had spent my time in 2017 being upset, instead of preparing myself for bigger and better things in 2018?

Every year when the SXSW festival comes around, I tweet about not letting FOMO get to you. Whether you've missed out on going and you're reading the tweets of people there, or you're attending the festival and you know you can't be everywhere at once, it can be easy to fall into the trap of FOMO. Every party at SXSW has some kind of after-party, with some kind of VIP section. If you're in the VIP section, you'll find out that there is a VVIP section. There is always some "better thing" that you can feel you are missing out on. Living in LA puts me at a really interesting intersection of entertainment, tech, and other types of wealth and status, so I've experienced some of these VIP areas at different points in my life. When I was writing my blog *Your Daily Lesbian Moment,* I would be ushered to the front of the line in certain lesbian clubs in LA. When working in the music industry, I always had a backstage pass. In tech, I've often been the keynote speaker at events. I have been behind the velvet ropes, and trust me, it isn't as exciting as it seems. The backstage pass, the VIP area, the secret after-party — all of this means nothing to me if I can't share it with others.

A lot of what happens in Silicon Valley comes from a place of FOMO. Everyone wants to be in on the next big thing, and everyone is terrified of being the investor that said no and missed out on a huge payout. Maybe I don't fear that because I don't chase unicorns; I invest in companies I believe in, companies that I want to succeed and that I can see having a positive impact on the world. I know the money will follow. When you make a decision, try to really take the time to work out what it is that is driving you. If your choices are being influenced by FOMO, there's a good chance you could be losing sight of your actual goals. Instead, you have to concentrate on yourself. You have to know yourself — you have to know what you want, what your version of success will look like — and then use that to decide if missing out is such a bad thing after all. Trust your instincts. I don't need to know what everyone else is doing to know what I want to do. I don't need to know what the biggest, coolest party is. I know that wherever I choose to be, that's the best deal, meeting, or party in town — for me. Following that feeling will take you far.

CHAPTER 22

SUCCESS IS MEANT TO BE SHARED

What does success look like when it's shared with others? What does success look like when you extend it to communities? How can you work toward creating a successful, empowered community? Who succeeds when you succeed? These are questions I thought about when I started Backstage Capital. I needed to decide between being a founder and using my knowledge to get into the boys' club of Silicon Valley, or starting my own fund and investing in hundreds of other underestimated founders. As time has passed, this question has come back to me again and again: **Who wins**

when I win? If I do well as a venture capitalist, then my investors also do well — that's how the system works.

As I found more and more ways to invest in those I truly believed in, I began to wonder about the people making money from my successes. When I imagine these businesses successful and thriving, I also imagine who is making gains from them. Who do I want to be sharing the upside of this with? Do I really want to make a few more wealthy, white men even richer than they already are? How does adding another zero to the end of their net worth change the ecosystem? I'm investing in companies led by underrepresented founders, and by doing that, I'm changing the landscape of start-ups. But could I be doing more for my community, the people who inspire me every day and challenge me to do better and be better?

Backstage headliner Denise Woodard founded Partake Foods in 2016, after her daughter was diagnosed with multiple food allergies. The company was created with the belief that sharing food and eating with others builds deep connections. It was important to Woodard that everyone — even those with food allergies and other dietary needs — should be able to partake in the ritual of eating together, and so she began creating delicious snacks that would be enjoyed by those with dietary restrictions as well as those without.

I met her at a pitch competition in North Carolina in 2017. It was during a mentoring session, and I was instantly blown away by two things: (1) her incredibly impressive résumé and breadth of experience, and (2) the fact that she was having a terrible time finding investors to believe in her. I invested the next day.

When she created this company, she thought further than "How can I create a product for people with allergies?" Woodard wanted this to be an inclusive company, so she considered the ways in which having an allergy could affect other parts of one's life. In addition to the fact that allergy-safe food was not readily available in most stores, it was expensive when it was available. For low-income families already struggling to get by, or people living in food deserts, getting allergy-safe products could be nearly impossible. Woodard decided to partner with organizations such as No Kid Hungry so that struggling families could have access to allergy-safe products as well as receive education about these foods. Partake Foods has partnered with more than seventy-five different nonprofit organizations and continues to add to that number each year.

Meanwhile, Woodard has been sharing information about other plant-based and eco-friendly companies for those customers who are looking to make a change in their diet due to climate or welfare concerns rather than health.

In doing this, the company helps other companies to grow alongside them and creates a community of like-minded people. Partake partners only with companies that share their ethics, meaning that their consumers trust their opinion and are more likely to engage with these companies. Through the blog on their website, they share recipes that can be made using Partake's products, post gift guides that cater to those looking to shop at small Black-owned businesses and/or environmentally friendly companies, and offer suggestions for affordable family activities. Partake has also partnered with bigger companies such as Ben & Jerry's, who are renowned for their dedication to justice movements.

Woodard thought about how to share her success with the communities she found herself in — both a small community of founders and entrepreneurs of color, and a community of Black and Asian American citizens working in the food and beverage industry. In 2020 she founded the Black Futures in Food & Beverage Fellowship to help HBCU students who would like to work in the industry. The annual program seeks to increase opportunities for underrepresented people through workshops, panels with leaders of industry, internships, and job offers.

In 2023 Partake Foods became a Certified B Corporation, meaning they have been certified by the organization

B Lab as a company dedicated to making a positive social and environmental impact. By becoming a B Corporation, Partake Foods has made a public promise to consider more than just their own profits.

This is what it looks like when you share your success with your community.

When I first started learning about venture capital from the outside, it just looked like it was designed to make a few specific people very rich and very powerful, and everybody else was like a cog, just a means to an end. In that ecosystem, the people who were getting the crumbs were Black people, women, LGBTQ+ people — all the same groups who were normally left out of things. I was really disheartened by that. Finally, I reached an inflection point where I said, "Wow, okay. I have three options, really. One option is that I can be really upset about this — really pissed, frustrated, etc. — and I can just give up and say, 'Who wants to be in that world anyway? Eff it, and I'll go and do this other music stuff instead.' A second option is that I could learn as much as I can and figure out how to be that one — call it the token, if you will — that gets in and gets to sit at the cool kids' table as long as they sit quietly and are acceptable to the system and don't get kicked out. The third option is to eff both of those — I can get a seat at the cool kids' table but do it my way and bring everybody with me." That's what I decided to do. Of course, we built several other, cooler tables.

My outlandish success is my activism — it's my fist in the air — because I aim to use my wins to catalyze others to do the same. If I can make Backstage Capital's mission obsolete, I will consider that a success.

CHAPTER 23

TRUE SUCCESS IS MEASURED NOT IN WORDS BUT IN ACTIONS

In 2020, the United States had its so-called racial reckoning following the murder of George Floyd. For a period of time, large corporations were actively thinking about their Black customers, their Black employees, and how they could ensure that they landed on the right side of history. This was carried out with mixed success; for some companies a blacked-out Instagram post and platitudes were all they were willing to give, while others made promises regarding diversity figures or established funds for Black business owners and entrepreneurs. As a Black woman I could say a lot about the failures of corporations during this time, but much has already been written by experts; my expertise is in venture funding, so I will concentrate on that.

Let me tell you, I had so many people reaching out to me in the summer of 2020. I was contacted by media outlets, venture capitalists, banks, corporations. Everyone wanted to know my opinion on investing in Black founders. Well, my opinion has always been out there for anyone to read—I believe Black founders and founders of color are worthy of investment, not as a good deed, not as a diversity checkbox, and not as a PR stunt. Throughout my career I have banged this drum. When race came to the forefront of everyone's attention and fund managers suddenly began to look around and see that they weren't hiring a diverse workforce, nor were they investing in a diverse range of founders, and they began to speak these truths out loud, I did think perhaps we were on our way to some real change. The people I'd been trying to convince for years to invest in Black founders, to take meetings with Black founders, and to take Black founders seriously—those same people who had told me the problem was one of "the pipeline," that there just weren't that many Black founders out there—those people seemed to have woken up. A lot of them seemed truly dismayed to realize that no matter their good intentions, they were part of a larger problem.

Something I think people misunderstand about me is my intentionality and thoughtfulness when it comes to speaking out. I think about what I post and who I talk about on Twitter and other social networks. I think very carefully about the words that I use and the effect that they could have. I know what it's like when you call someone out. It comes with a lot of blowback from a lot of people, and most of the time I'm not interested in dealing with that. But there are also things that I feel are very important to speak out about, and speaking my truth — and telling it how it is — is how my career in venture began. So while I know I'll get some backlash for speaking about this again, it bears repeating that even at the height of the racial reckoning, some of the largest venture capital firms did very little and expected a lot of praise.

Andreessen Horowitz, for example — a top VC firm based out of California — announced that they would be providing a $2.2 million fund for Black founders, and they expected to be cheered for that. I felt like it was just one more insult added to the years of insult and injury working in this sector. That amount — $2.2 million — is a large amount of money; it would be the kind of money I would aim for with a Backstage fund, and it's the kind of money we have scraped together from LPs (limited partners, one of those being Marc Andreessen himself) to do our early-stage investing. It will no doubt be very impactful for the founders who receive a percentage of it. But Andreessen Horowitz has tens of billions of dollars under management. They could have created a fund of $200 million and it would barely have even made a dent in their overall investing budget. Knowing what they could do versus what they chose to do was an insult. It proved that we were not being taken seriously, that we were not a priority, even in that heightened moment and the public scrutiny that came with it.

I'm not here to cast blame on any individual people who work for these funds. I have a lot of respect and appreciation for many of them. So I'll tell you exactly what I told Nait Jones, who got in touch with me after I spoke out about Andreessen Horowitz. Nait (a Black man) was overseeing this $2.2 million fund at the time and wanted to let me know that he was upset with me for putting down his work. I said to him, "I don't minimize your work. I know how hard it must be when you're working within such a large organization to get any attention to these issues and I appreciate it. I'm upset with your bosses. I'm upset with the powers that be. I get to do that — I have the moral high ground to stand on — because I've put all of my blood, sweat, and tears into raising this kind of capital for early-stage funding, with none of the money or contacts behind me that a huge fund like Andreessen Horowitz has." But I don't want to put Nait Jones down. I want Nait Jones to win; I want him to be able to oversee a much larger fund for underestimated founders. He's just one example, and he may disagree with me. Remember: we contain multitudes.

In June of 2020, Sequoia Capital, another hugely wealthy investment company, posted a message on Twitter that they had sent out to their team; in it they condemned racism, violence, bigotry, and hate. They offered counseling to their employees and agreed to match employee donations to civil rights organizations two to one. They emphasized the importance and power of individual actions. What they didn't mention was anything about how they would improve the diversity of their own company or ensure that Black founders were getting an equal chance at investment.

I called them out, and I said what I thought: Sequoia couldn't care less, just as most funds couldn't care less. They'll continue to succeed because they're too big to fail. Alfred Lin, a partner at Sequoia, got in touch with me and asked me what he could do to make things right and fix this. I told him: "Take the millions and billions of dollars in capital and management fees that the fund makes and hire Black professionals. Offer them whatever you can to bring them in. There are people out there who are doing the work right now; you do not have to wring your hands — it's laid out for you!" He told me that it takes a long time for change to happen within the walls of a big fund like theirs and that it might take time but he would try. I haven't seen it happen yet, but who knows.

There are many more examples of companies still hiding behind the excuse of the pipeline. I'm not buying it. Anyone who says there aren't enough Black founders to invest in isn't doing their job, which is to look at all the founders applying to be part of their fund and investing in the best ones. That's all we are asking. If you're truly doing your job right, some of those founders will be Black, and you won't have had to change your investment thesis or lower your standards. You'll simply have done your job.

The bottom line? Simply saying that we believe in something is meaningless if we do only the bare minimum to act on it. True success and true impact aren't measured in words; they are measured in actions.

Exercises

+ Think about the notion of success and write down what you think success looks like. Note what you have been working toward, how you have been measuring your wins and your misses, and what you would need to be successful if you stuck to that definition.

- Consider who it is that you measure yourself against. Are there things they have achieved that you want for yourself? Have you achieved something that they haven't? Is it a fair comparison?

- Next, take a step back and look at the bigger picture of your life. Take stock of your financial situation, your social situation, the things you love about your life, and the parts that feel emptier. Consider what is important to you. Think about your goals. Make a list of what you want.

- Now it's time for your action plan. What steps can you take to get you closer to that life you want? What can you do right now, and what can you do in six months? Start thinking in actionable steps.

PART FIVE

CATALYZING

Fast Company put me on the front cover of their magazine in October of 2018, with the headline "Venture Catalyst." I love that they chose this headline because every day I wake up with my eyes on the prize of catalyzing others. Before every decision I make, I ask myself: *What does this change? Who could be affected by this?* When I'm looking at companies to invest in, through Backstage Capital or personally, I ask myself: *What is impactful globally, with this company and that company? What changes the game? What changes lives?* Many of the companies in our portfolio are changing and saving lives, and that is both important and exhilarating. When you invest in companies whose work you really believe in, you want them to win for so many more reasons than just a return on investment.

Everything I do is about inflection points. If I meet you where lightning strikes and I can do something in that moment that will accelerate you, I will do that. I will do that at scale. When a few underestimated people succeed in a big way, it makes everyone feel good for a while; it lets us believe we're making progress, even though for the other 99.9% of us, things remain exactly the same. I'm not interested in creating the illusion of change. I'm interested in blowing up the whole system, and there is never just one part to my plan. I'm always thinking ahead about what to do next, what I could change, and what the ripple effects might be. I don't want to look up in ten years' time to see that the same groups of people I'm investing in now are still underestimated. I don't want to see the route to capital, or to financial success, still littered with the same obstacles I've had to climb over and push through. I want this to be easier for future generations.

Structural inequalities mean some groups of people have an easier time becoming wealthy. Period. I want to change this. I want a redistribution of wealth that smooths the rough edges we've been bumping up against our whole lives. I can't change history, but every time I catalyze an underestimated person, I get the opportunity to change the future. More importantly, *they* get the opportunity to change the future. Investing in people can turn lives around. If we can keep investing in underestimated founders, if we can keep proving they can deliver just as much and more when someone believes in them, we can create generational wealth for families who have never had that.

When I was poor, I wanted to be rich. Money is

something I thought about a lot, even when I was a kid. My mom and I had to think about money all the time because we lacked it. I was like an adult co-running the house with my mother long before I was a legal adult, and constantly thinking about how much something was going to cost and could we afford it was part of that. Now that I am growing into wealth, I don't think about money as something I need to survive — I think of it as a tool to help uplift others, to help bring about the change I want to see in the world. I no longer have reverence for it; I just want to use it to improve our society. Some of that impact I won't see in my lifetime — and I'm fine with that. As my mother quotes, "Sometimes the seed doesn't see the petal." I'm aiming to leave behind the most beautiful garden.

If you take one thing from this book, I hope that it's this: You don't have to be rich to plant the seeds for that beautiful garden. **You don't have to be born into a legacy of wealth to leave a legacy behind.** Influence can come in many forms. It could mean giving money (e.g., being a customer of a local business or using a service regularly and leaving a tip), it could mean giving time (e.g., sitting on the PTA of your kid's school or joining an employee resource group at your company), or it could mean giving advice (e.g., advising a friend or mentoring a colleague). Or it could simply mean giving someone the chance to do the thing they're good at (e.g., hiring someone who doesn't yet have a lot of experience so that they can gain that experience with you). Once you start thinking about the things you do every day that affect other people, you will probably find that this is a long list; our sphere of influence is usually so much larger than we realize.

You can change lives using the tools you already have as long as you're intentional about what you're doing. I catalyze in multiple ways: through investing, education, scholarships, mentorship, representation, and transparency — through pulling up not just one chair, but as many chairs as I can. When I invest in a company, I don't invest just money. I invest time, ideas, and energy.

It's important to think about your role in your community and decide how you can make the most impact. It may be that you are an influential voice or that you have time you can give to make a process easier for someone else. We all have things we can give — we have talents that are useful or friends in other industries who we can connect to others. Sometimes donating money is the least impactful thing you can do. It all comes down to the situation and each of us as individuals. Ask yourself: *What can I offer aside from money?*

CHAPTER 24

INVEST IN IMPACT

B y August of 2020, I was exhausted. In June of that year, TechCrunch had requested a comment for an article about all these venture capital firms suddenly making noise about supporting Black founders. I gave out my email address in the article and told these firms that if they wanted a curated list of Black founders to invest in or Black investors to hire, they could reach out to me. Two months later, I was sick and tired of the bloviations and the lies from the vast majority of institutional investors and large corporations that had gotten in touch; only a tiny percentage of the emails and calls I had received had turned into actual opportunities. Again, I thought long and hard about who it was that I wanted to share my success with, who I wanted to feel the impact of my work. That's when I decided that I wanted to move Backstage Capital away from relying on traditional venture capital investments. Not because I couldn't raise money that way; I'd raised millions of dollars through venture capital at that point. But did I *want* to keep doing it that way? Frankly, I was tired of feeling like I was begging for scraps from the industry.

I often talk about the whiteboard I had when I was still learning about investing. I'd written KEEP GOING on it in permanent marker, and I think of that message often. What I haven't spoken about as much is the other message I wrote to myself, which was WE DON'T BEG. I'm good at raising capital. I can be persuasive and confident and convincing, because I truly believe in the companies I want to invest in and I truly believe in the mission I'm on. But the more time I've spent convincing other people of the legitimacy of these companies and the bright future we're working toward, the more I've thought, *Do I really want to share my success with people I have to work so hard to convince? Is that person investing in the company because they believe in its potential or because I talked them into it?* I decided that I didn't want to spend my time chasing down this funding. Instead, I wanted to take the opportunities that I was throwing at rich investors and find a way to share them with people who saw the potential from the beginning.

It was this train of thought that led me to think about crowdfunding as a way to give more people access to investment opportunities. We wanted everyone to know that you don't have to have hundreds of thousands of dollars to spare to be an impact investor, that investing in change is within reach, and that you don't need to wait for anyone to invite you to the party. We set up Backstage Crowd so that both accredited and unaccredited investors could invest in companies and people that they believe in.

Backstage Crowd is a syndicate, meaning that it joins forces with other investors to put money into businesses. Backstage Crowd uses the deal flow we amass through Backstage Capital and presents certain deals to investors on terms they would not have access to otherwise.

Setting up Backstage Crowd wasn't easy. There were a lot of legal hoops to jump through, and like anything that is new or innovative, we had to create our own blueprint. We decided it had to be done — it needed to exist — and so we built it.

There are a lot of laws and rules around investing services, some of which are very important and designed to protect the average person, and some of which have been in need of an update for a long time. As I mentioned previously, when we launched Backstage Crowd, the SEC considered accredited investors to be people who made $200,000 in annual income as an individual (or $300,000 in annual income with a spouse) or who had at least one million dollars in personal assets (not including their permanent home). Obviously, this cut out a lot of people. Anyone who didn't have this kind of income or assets was an unaccredited investor, and there were (and still are) strict rules about what they can and cannot invest in.

Many of these rules were created to protect regular people from being taken advantage of in the financial market, which is understandable, but at the same time, what these rules are saying is that if you don't have a lot of money in your bank account, you shouldn't have the agency to make your own decisions. Here we see the same tired bias toward wealthy people in play. It's assumed that if you make more than a certain amount of money, you are knowledgeable about finance and investing, but if you don't make that amount, you need to be protected from yourself. Meanwhile, any person over eighteen can go to a casino and blow hundreds of thousands of dollars gambling every weekend but can't take that same money and invest it into a company they believe in. Why is one okay and not the other?

Unaccredited investors are worthy investors, yet there are still all kinds of rules and regulations around the kind of funds that they can invest in. Meanwhile, I know plenty of people who have worked within the financial industry and built their career investing other people's money but didn't make enough to qualify as accredited. Before Backstage Crowd even existed, I began working with the SEC, along with other investors, to change some of these rules to make investing more equitable. In 2019, the SEC announced that investors could qualify as accredited if they had professional knowledge, either through experience or certifications.

We launched the Backstage Crowd syndicate because we wanted to empower as many investors as possible to get involved with companies that weren't always getting their fair share of attention. More than anything, we wanted to share some of the future upside of these companies with the people who truly believed in them.

The first deal that we took to Backstage Crowd was for Akash Systems, which sends satellites into space. The community raised $500,000 in two weeks. It became the largest individual investment we had ever made, and it proved the idea that we don't have to rely on just one or two people with power and resources. Together, we can pool our resources and create our own power.

The success of Backstage Crowd showed us that if we could bring lots of people together to raise money for other companies Backstage was supporting, we could also do the same for Backstage itself. This time, we used a platform called Republic to fund our operations costs. I knew there were hundreds if not thousands of people out there who believed in Backstage Capital. They just weren't necessarily millionaires. I started to wonder what Backstage Capital would look like if it belonged to all of us. I'd never seen a fund looking for investment in this way, but as I always say, "If it doesn't exist, let's create it." I had to imagine it and then we had to create the path to make it fruitful, legal, and compliant.

The public would be offered a chance to own part of Backstage Umbrella, LLC, which housed Backstage Capital and the accelerator programs we had previously invested in. The minimum investment was $100, and whether you invested $100 or $100,000, you were an owner of Backstage Umbrella and had access to all of the same information.

When we launched the campaign, in February of 2021, the most we were legally allowed to raise was $1.07 million. We raised that in eight hours. We were blown away by the public's enthusiasm. We started taking names for a waiting list so that the next time we raised, those on the waiting list could get in first. In March of 2021, the SEC changed the maximum amount we could legally raise to $5 million. We reopened the round, and in seven days, we hit the target and became the first-ever venture fund to crowdfund for $5 million for operations costs in the United States.

We currently have more than six thousand investors. When I wake up in the morning and think about how I will make money for my investors, I'm motivated by that number. I'm fired up by the idea that if I win, more than six thousand other people also win. More than six thousand people believed in the values and ethos of Backstage as a company enough to bet on us and to bet on themselves. For me, the most exciting thing is the idea that in ten years' time, I'll be able to look back on an impressive portfolio owned by thousands of stakeholders. The profits will be shared by all of them. This is impact in action.

CHAPTER 25

KNOCK DOWN THE STAIRWAY AND BUILD AN ELEVATOR

We cannot catalyze change if we take our gains and ignore those we leave behind. Always be thinking of the "we" and the "us," not the "I" and the "me." When you're invited to sit at the table, make sure you pull out a chair for someone else.

I never want to be the one exception. When you know the struggle of being underestimated or being oppressed, you have to use that knowledge to knock down the stairway and build an elevator.

One of the people I admire who lives up to this ideal is Liz Fong-Jones. Liz invested in Backstage Capital back in 2018. Liz is a talented software-developer advocate, labor and ethics organizer, and site reliability engineer (SRE) who has worked in the tech industry for well over a decade. She invests in for-profit companies that are social impact–focused, provides grants for nonprofit organizations, and has lent her knowledge to the National Center for Transgender Equality by sitting on their board. When she originally reached out to me about investing in Backstage Capital, she told me that she wanted to spend her money on things that moved forward the activism, actions, and dignity of LGBTQ+ folks and especially the transgender community. When I interviewed her on my podcast (episode 3), she explained the hypothesis behind her investments and donations:

"No one becomes a multimillionaire without choosing to. . . . I think it would be horrendous for me to accumulate a bunch of wealth and just keep it all to myself rather than using it for the good of the community, because for every person like me, there are plenty of people who are struggling."[*] Everything she does comes back to the same

---

[*] Arlan Hamilton and Liz Fong-Jones, "You *Can* Be Successful as a Trans Person. I Wish There Were More of Us," June 8, 2019, in *Your First Million*, produced by Anna Eichenauer and Bryan Landers, podcast, https://podcasts .apple.com/us/podcast/your-first-million/id1467515562?i=1000441183764.

question: "How do I both help cultivate the next generation of trans folks to survive, but thrive as well and to also be able to give back to the community? I aim to spend my money to maximize impact," she said.

Due to her own experience as a transgender woman of color, Liz focuses on the problems faced by this group in all areas of their lives, from policy work to poverty to harassment. This is her North Star. Like me, Liz did not come from a wealthy background, and she sees the money she now has as a tool she can use to impact her community. In her mind, to *not* use that tool would be like walking past someone crying out for help and ignoring them.

Beyond her investing and grant-making, Liz also creates impact by being a vocal transgender woman talking openly about money. She knows it's important that people see a successful trans person in the world, noting that people need to recognize that "there is somewhere in between the Caitlyn Jenners of the world and the trans folks who are struggling to make rent."

Being the representation we need in the world can be a really powerful way of catalyzing others. When you're looking for someone to emulate and you can't find anyone you can relate to, take that as a sign that **the person you're looking for might be you.** Don't let the lack of representation put you off. If you need that role model and can't find it, you can be certain there are others out there also searching for that person. In the same way, if you have an idea and you're being told it can't be done, don't let that stop you. You have to face the 15% of dissenting people if you are going to do something audacious. If it were easy to do, everyone would have already done it. Sometimes, you have to be the one to blaze the trail, then light the path for others to follow.

CHAPTER 26

THE POWER OF GIVING POWER TO OTHERS

I met Mark Cuban in 2019 when I was approached by Twitter to speak at the SXSW festival in Austin. Twitter had also asked Mark to appear on their house stage, and they wanted us to interview each other. Though we'd never officially met, I felt as though I'd known of Mark for a long time. I loved watching *Shark Tank* and found myself often agreeing with his comments. Even before I founded Backstage Capital, I used to watch the TV show and pretend I was the fifth shark. We also both have a Dallas connection. I grew up in Dallas and still consider it my hometown, and Mark owns the Dallas

Mavericks of the NBA and has come to have a big influence there.

To this day I have no idea whether Mark knew anything about me before we were booked together, but I definitely had some preconceived notions about him. I thought, *Well, he's a billionaire. So he's probably going to roll deep. He'll probably have an entourage. He probably won't be so easy to talk to.* I've been in that situation a lot — meeting someone famous and feeling like I'm meeting the queen because there is so much fanfare around the person. Sometimes these people roll with an entourage for physical protection, and sometimes it's for social protection and companionship, while other times it's for the ego boost. Whatever the reason, when you meet someone like that, you don't always know what you're going to get. So I thought to myself, *Who knows? Maybe Mark Cuban's a jerk. Maybe he's not interesting, or maybe I meet him, we have a conversation onstage, he walks away, and I never see him again,* because that has happened multiple times too, and the person wasn't always a billionaire.

But it turned out that Mark was nothing at all like I expected. One of the first things I noticed about him is that when I saw him in the backstage area, I had more people with me than he did. My mom, my brother, my makeup artist, and one other person had come with me, and he, as far as I could see, had arrived solo. He was sitting in a chair by himself, and I walked over to him and introduced myself. I don't know if he had just been briefed on me, but he immediately said, "Oh, you're from Dallas. That's great. Love what you're doing with Backstage."

I introduced him to my mom and my brother, and he chatted with them and took photos with my brother, who is a big Dallas sports fan. I asked him a couple of questions before we went onstage, to warm up, as I still wasn't sure what to expect. I asked him if being constantly pitched by people ever got on his nerves, or if he felt bored after having heard thousands and thousands of pitches over the years and having invested in hundreds of companies. He had this big boyish grin on his face, and he said, "No, not in a million years can I get tired of this, would this ever get boring to me. I just love it so much. I love entrepreneurship. I love new businesses. I love the hunt, the competition, all of it." I recognized in him the same insatiable curiosity that I have and the same love for the energy and excitement of it all.

The event went really well and I contacted Mark afterward, by direct message on Twitter, to ask if he would be interested in investing in Backstage Capital. He said no and explained that he doesn't like investing in funds, as he's much more interested in companies. I understood his point of view and I respected it. I'm used to hearing no, and it was much more thoughtful than most of the rejections I get. It made sense, and I thought that was that.

A few weeks later, Dan Primack of Axios wrote an article about me that was not flattering and, in my opinion, not accurate. The article claimed that I had failed in my mission to raise a $36 million fund to invest in start-ups led by Black women and that people in the industry had given me too much credit too early. I don't spend a whole lot of time worrying about what people think about me, but when someone says something publicly that hurts my business and in turn all the employees and founders who depend on it, that's a different story. In this case, a lot of industry professionals read the article, or even just saw the headline, and made a decision about me based on that. That was when Mark reached out to me privately, out of the blue, and said, "Hey, I'm going to invest a million dollars in you. Let's help you build some wealth, so that you don't have to worry about looking for money from the outside."

To give context, most of Backstage Capital's LPs each had invested anywhere from $25,000 to $250,000 at that point. There had been only one person who had invested up to a million dollars over time, and it was incredibly impactful — perhaps more so than anything I can think of, besides my first check. But for Mark to come to me and say, "Here is a million dollars — you can invest it in whatever you want," without giving me any hoops to jump through, and with no expectation of publicity, was so important and spoke volumes. The article framed the situation with our fund as a personal failure of mine, when really it was a failure of infrastructure. Mark understood this and was reacting to the situation by looking at how he could use his money to lift me up. He used his power to give me power.

In May of 2020, Mark reached out again and said, "Ready to do more? I want to put $5 million more into what you're doing." At that time, a lot of people, and a lot of companies, were wringing their hands and looking for ways to show their horror and allyship in the wake of George Floyd's death. But once again, what Mark did was private and intentional. He wasn't doing it because of how it would look but because it was a way he could catalyze change, and so he went ahead and did it without a press release or a statement to the media. He told me, "Okay, you'll get up to a million dollars every quarter. Same thing, $100,000 deals, unless you think there's something that should be different." He also offered me 30% carry (profit share), which is an industry high.

So by 2021, Mark Cuban had invested a third or so of that $5 million. Although he was happy for me to make the investing decisions myself, he also let me know that he was available if I had any questions. Sometimes I would email him about deals we were considering, just to get his feedback, and we didn't always agree. In fact, we've had multiple disagreements about whether or not to invest in a company, but he always nurtured a fair fight. I would think he was wrong, and he would think I was wrong, and that was okay, because he empowered me to do things my own way, even in those cases where we didn't see eye to eye.

Mark gave me power in another way too. His involvement in the fund — indirectly, at least — opened the door to investments from other powerful people: Serena Williams invested in a seed round for Mahmee, the maternal health company, alongside Mark and me. I was leading the multimillion-dollar round because of the relationship I had already built with the founders. Mark put in substantially more money personally, and Serena put in money and also lent credibility due to her own experience with childbirth, which was invaluable.

One of the reasons you want to be around millionaires and billionaires is to learn from them, but another reason is proximity. You can earn power and leverage just from being close to certain systems and people. Being able to make the phone call, having access to people who can make things happen — all of that is powerful. Once you get access to some of that power, it's up to you to share it with others.

CHAPTER 27

CATALYZE LEARNING

I think of my modes of catalyzing as four pillars: one pillar is **investing,** another is **execution,** another is **amplification,** and the final pillar is the **education** part. They're all linked. I'm trying to move a boulder representing the past four hundred years of history and the past seventy years of venture — it takes a lot of different levers to lift that weight.

In 2018, I visited Oxford in the United Kingdom for the first time when I was asked to speak at Oxford Foundry, the entrepreneurship center at Oxford University's business school. As I toured the beautifully manicured university grounds, I didn't see much diversity as I walked around, so I asked the tour guide, "Where are the Black people?" They were few and far between. When I thought about the distinguished history and reputation of the institution, I couldn't help but wish that more people like me could have that experience. After my forty-five-minute tour ended, I said, "I want to start a scholarship for Black students."

I could imagine it in my mind's eye: I wanted someone who wouldn't have otherwise had the opportunity to go to Oxford to have the chance to go. I wanted them not to have to worry about the things I've had to worry about in the past, like how to pay rent, tuition, or bills. I wanted them to be able to get the kind of education that would fuel them in whatever way, to go out and kick some butt, and then to pay it forward. I returned a few months later and made it official.

We decided not to put a mandate on what the student studies at Oxford and also to offer them the ability to work at the foundry's start-up accelerator, which I advise. Students apply for the scholarship through the university, not through me, so I'm quite hands-off; I don't decide who gets it and I don't decide what they study. My mother always taught me that when you give someone a gift, you give it to them and then it's theirs to do what they want with it.

My mother, Earline Sims, majored in psychology at Dillard University, an HBCU in New Orleans. She's always talked about how important a time it was in her life and how much she loved her experiences there. So we decided we would set up a scholarship there together. She asked that the scholarship be for a student who wanted to study psychology, someone like her younger self.

As I write this, I have given nearly one million dollars in scholarship money to various people since 2019. Beyond the direct impact, I hope it will be an example that inspires other people to do something similar. A few months after that first trip to Oxford, Robert Smith, an engineer and investor who also happens to be the richest Black person in America, paid off the student debt for an entire graduating class of Morehouse College students, which was a baller move. At the time, he said something along the lines of "Don't let me be the only person to do this," and I take that very seriously. For me, this isn't just about giving the student who wins the scholarship an opportunity — it's about catalyzing that student to go on and be successful and also set up a scholarship. The Oxford scholarship is the very first one in the history of Oxford University that is specifically for a Black student. I hope it's the first of many.

After I announced the Oxford scholarship, a lot of people reached out to me asking for sponsorship. One of them stood out — a young Black woman in the UK who was studying to be a pilot. She was halfway through her studies and falling behind with her payments, because even though she and her mother had been working sixteen hours a day to pay the school fees, they just weren't able to keep up with the costs.

Between tour managing and working at Backstage Capital, I've probably flown on a thousand flights. In 2018, I traveled so much that I was away from home for roughly three hundred days of the year, *and yet, I have never seen a Black female pilot.* I've seen a female pilot two times and a Black male pilot once. So to me, this young student was a true unicorn — and I had to invest in her! She caught my attention because I'm always going to believe that we should be represented everywhere and because I could see the impact in both the immediate and not-so-immediate future: the immediate impact being that she wouldn't have to quit her studies after getting so far, and the future impact being that she could go on to inspire others as an example of a Black female pilot in a world where people like her are so few and far between. When she asked how she could pay me back, I told her I was hoping that one day I'll be on a flight and she'll be the pilot.

In June of 2021, I watched the viral video of Paxton Smith giving the valedictorian speech at my old high school, Lake Highlands High School, in Texas. Following the school's policy, she had given a copy of her speech to school administrators in advance of graduation day, but she also had a rogue speech prepared — a passionate, powerful one, all about abortion rights. She was obviously nervous, as she knew there was a reasonable chance she would be booed or kicked offstage, but the message was so important to her that she gave the speech anyway. It was so cool to see something like that happen at my old high school. Paxton took a big personal risk to make a statement about something she felt very strongly about and ended up reaching millions of people with her message. Sadly, three months later the Texas abortion ban was passed. But I felt her bravery should be celebrated, so I reached out to her and got to know her and her family a little. I thought to myself, *This is a person with the potential to not only make a true impact on the world but also to catalyze that impact in others.* So, to ensure that she was able to continue on with her education, I created a scholarship fund for her.

This is the kind of stuff I can do while still in the game — hustling and earning money so that I can give money where and when I want.

While I believe that college can be very valuable for many, I also believe there are other, equally valuable ways for people to get an education. Since day 1 of Backstage Capital, I knew I wanted to have an **apprenticeship** program, for people like my younger self who are looking for a way to get into the industry, to learn from someone who is doing it, and to get some experience on their résumé. So many apprenticeships have always felt quite closed and opaque; they seemed to be another situation in which it was more about who you knew and your ability to pay than your eagerness to learn. So I did some research about other programs and thought back to my own experience taking a course in 2015, and in 2021, I launched an official program. In that first year, I accepted twenty-one apprentices who had previously been students of my Investing as a Catalyst course. Originally the program ran for four months, with two virtual meetings a week. I was always at one of the two meetings, and people could ask me anything they wanted to. They also had hands-on training with the Backstage team and got to read through deals, discuss them and score them, and make determinations.

I thought it would be a really cool thing to be able to offer them a piece of Backstage Capital — to give them a small ownership stake in the company. I decided that it was important to show that I really mean it when I say I'm dedicated to sharing the wealth. You can talk about it all you want, but at some point you have to show it with your wallet. I offered the apprentices the chance to split 1% of Backstage Capital among them. This meant that at the current valuation, I was giving them the chance to own a piece of Backstage worth $25,000 each! This is something that would usually be reserved for a company's senior executive who was hired within the first three months.

Offering an apprenticeship doesn't have to cost you

anything more than time. You can offer your experience, mentorship, and advice, and the time you spend investing in the apprentice may well be rewarded in the form of an experienced and well-trained person you can hire in the future.

The more underrepresented people I support, the more underrepresented people there are in the field for other underrepresented people to look up to. Being underrepresented is something I want to put an end to. I want us represented in every industry, in every important room, and at every important table. Why shouldn't we be? This is why it is essential to catalyze representation in the start-up and investment ecosystem in a meaningful way.

Another way to do this is through **transparency.** Being transparent about what we're doing is kind of like offering a mini apprenticeship, at scale. By being transparent about what I'm working on, what I'm finding hard, and how often I choose to prioritize rest, I am letting others read the manual. When I started my company Runner, I chose to build it from the ground up in public. That meant keeping the public updated on what we were doing behind the scenes as well as through the usual PR. Through my podcast *Your First Million,* listeners can hear about all of the important milestones we reach at Runner, as well as any failures we have. I'm willing to fail in public because I think it's important for people to see that part of the journey.

Runner could fail, and if we do, we'll look at what went wrong and we'll learn from it. If that happens, I want all my listeners to learn from it too. I'm on a learning curve, and I'm bringing everyone with me.

When you dare to share what you're doing, and you put yourself out there for others to see, you encourage people to think big, take chances, and, if they fail, do it publicly so others can learn from their mistakes. If you change one person's outlook, that's a win.

When I started recording my podcast, I thought, *What if only a few people listen?* Then I reframed the question and asked, *What if a few people listen?* Having any audience at all is a privilege and an accomplishment. The thing to remember about producing content is that if you do so consistently, eventually there will be someone new discovering you and your content on a daily basis. That's a remarkable and powerful incentive. What if there is someone else around the world feeling the same way, struggling with the same challenges, and striving for the same goals as you are, and they come across your blog post or YouTube video or podcast? Something that seems normal and insignificant to you could have a huge impact on someone else; you dare to share yourself and they then feel seen or represented or heard. It doesn't end with you, and you never know which spark is going to light a fire.

Exercises

+ If you want to get involved in impact investing, the first step is deciding on your thesis: What makes you want to invest in something? What impact are you looking to have? What do you want the world to look like in five, ten, or twenty years? Let's say you're passionate about diversity, the environment, or health care — or some combination of the three. You could decide that 50% of your investments will go to founders in the health-care space, that 30% will go to Black founders committed to sustainable business practices, and that 10% will go toward companies building new tech aimed at older people. Anything that you're interested in can be part of your thesis, and if you have some previous knowledge of that industry or sector, you're coming in with an extra advantage. Most importantly, never invest more than you can afford to lose. If you don't have it now, you could make it a goal to put together a savings account.

+ Take some time to make a list of all the people, places, and things that you have any kind of influence on, whether it's the businesses where you shop, the groups in which you are a member, or the people in your life who come to you for advice. Remember that our sphere of influence is usually so much larger than we realize.

- Once you acknowledge the breadth of your influence, you can use it to catalyze positive change in the life of others. Think about the people in your orbit who you would like to help and what you have to offer them. Then consider how you could expand that sphere of influence.

CONCLUSION

There are few people in the world who have interviewed as many millionaires and billionaires as I have. In the past decade, I've researched, studied, and spoken with countless successful people who have reached their first million and beyond. I've learned three key lessons from this unique journey:

- **Almost anyone can become a millionaire.** Yes, that includes you. It doesn't matter where you're starting from, what setbacks you've encountered, or how many times you've been told it's impossible. Becoming a millionaire is within reach for those who dare to write their own headlines and, most important, act.

- **Millionaires do two things exceptionally well: they own things and they collaborate.** It's not just about earning a paycheck. True, sustainable wealth comes from ownership. Whether it's start-ups, real estate, stocks, or intellectual property, owning assets is key. Additionally, millionaires understand the power of collaboration. Whether they realize it or not, no millionaire is an island. Savvy ones harness the strengths, knowledge, and resources of others to catapult their own success.

- **The skills needed to become a millionaire from scratch *can* be taught.** You don't have to be born with a silver spoon, or be a genius, or get lucky at a casino. Through diligent learning, unwavering commitment, and the right guidance, you can acquire the skill set to climb to that million-dollar mark.

Here's why this is fantastic news for us:

First and foremost, these truths debunk the myth that wealth is reserved for the privileged few. Instead, they paint a picture of a democratized financial landscape, where ambition, learning, and perseverance are the true currency. It means that your past doesn't define your financial future. *You* do. As the subtitle of this book says, you don't have to be born into a legacy of wealth to leave one behind. Every decision, every risk taken, every lesson learned, plays a part in your unique journey to your first million.

Another reason for optimism is the knowledge that collaboration is an accelerant to wealth. And, hey, you already have some points on the board: by merely reading this book, you are collaborating with me! You're gaining insights from my experiences, mistakes, and triumphs. And remember, collaboration is reciprocal. As much as you learn from others, there's someone out there who can benefit from your unique insights and skills. That's the beauty of collaborative wealth building: it thrives on mutual growth.

Lastly, the teachable nature of wealth-building skills means that you have embarked on a transformative journey. Every strategy you've absorbed from this book is a step toward mastery. And while this text offers a road map, remember that my podcast, *Your First Million*, available in both video and audio formats, contains countless more gems. Real-life examples, candid conversations, and practical advice serve as breadcrumbs on your path to success.

You've equipped yourself with knowledge, but the real power lies in application. Your ambition, combined with the actionable insights from this book, can be the catalyst to not only achieve but also surpass that million-dollar mark.

I also recently reached my first million earned within a

calendar year and have thankfully repeated this since. I accomplished this via:

- **Speaking Engagements:** After overcoming debilitating stage fright, I have spoken at more than a hundred key events, sharing insights and connecting with diverse audiences.
- **Digital Courses:** I created and offered online courses to meet the learning needs of many.
- **Consulting:** I worked with entrepreneurs to offer solutions and guidance.
- **Publishing:** I sold two books (including the one you're reading) in six-figure deals that are paid out over time against sales.
- **Brand Sponsorships:** I partnered with brands, achieving shared goals and mutual benefits.

Remember, becoming a millionaire isn't just about the money; it's about the journey, the people you meet along the way, the communities you uplift, and the legacy you create. I truly hope that as you've flipped through these pages, you've found more than just financial strategies. I hope you've found hope, inspiration, and, most important, a renewed belief in your potential.

I look forward to hearing your success stories, witnessing your growth, and celebrating your milestones. Whether you're just starting or are well on your way, remember this: your first million is not a dream; it's a milestone waiting to be achieved. With determination, collaboration, and the right guidance, there's no limit to what you can accomplish.

Imagine the world a decade from now if we could catalyze the creation of a thousand new millionaires. Not just any millionaires, but individuals who reflect the true demographics of the United States. Think about the strength of that message — for every one billionaire, there are a thousand millionaires from different races, backgrounds, and genders. That's not just powerful; it's transformational.

A pivotal step to this vision as I see it is my first large-scale event series, Your First Million LIVE. Starting in April 2024 in Los Angeles, this isn't just another conference.

It's an electrifying gathering of dreamers and doers, bound by a common purpose.

Whether you're at the beginning of your entrepreneurial journey or you've already tasted success, this event promises to be a game changer. Mark your calendars and join me at YourFirstMillion.live.

In the pages of this book, I've shared tools, strategies, and insights. But the most important element, the real secret sauce, is you. Your drive, your ambition, your dream. That's the magic ingredient that will transform these tools into tangible success. Your passion will propel you to places you've only dreamed of.

The challenge is clear, and the goal is set. One thousand new millionaires, reflecting the true spirit and diversity of America. It's ambitious, even audacious. But I believe in us and in the vision of what we can achieve together.

As you move ahead, be fearless in your pursuit. Embrace challenges, learn from setbacks, and always keep the bigger picture in mind. The road to a million — and beyond — is paved with perseverance, resilience, and an unwavering belief in yourself.

INDEX

Index

Index

Index

Index

Index

Index

Index

Index

as company leaders, 7, 21, 35, 115, 116, 128, 163, 164, 170–73, 180
definition of success and, 152
empowerment of, 11, 62
failures of, 44
friends and family round and, 77, 78
fundraising rounds and, 76–78, 79
generational wealth and, 26, 92
geographic disparity and, 117
as hackers, 40
impostor syndrome and, 33
investments of, 62
mini empires and, 115, 116, 128
money as tool and, 13
networks and, 134
start-ups and, 27–28
success of, 179–80
venture capital industry and, 24, 25–26, 93
on wealth, 59
underrepresented communities
company founders and, 7, 10–11, 13, 24, 34, 36, 75, 77, 79, 164, 170–71
founders of companies and, 7, 10–11, 13, 24, 34, 36, 75, 77, 79, 164, 170–73
impostor syndrome and, 32, 33
local ecosystems and, 117–18
ownership and, 75
products and, 84–86
sharing success with, 166–67, 190–93
support for, 206
venture capital industry and, 23–25, 36, 167, 170–74, 183–84
wealth in, 13–14, 26–27

unemployment assistance, 37, 55
Unreal Estate. *See* Abode
Urgent Company, The, 126

Valley, The podcast, 69
values, and team building, 131
venture capital (VC)
Black women and, 23–24
fundraising and, 79–83, 88, 89–90, 93
LGBTQ+ community and, 23, 191
venture capital industry
applications for funding and, 75
collaboration and, 128
ecosystem of, 167–68
generational wealth and, 51
geographical disparity and, 117
Arlan Hamilton's dating site and, 9–10
income streams and, 66
management fees and, 94–96, 107
men's domination of, 10, 25
mini empires and, 120, 129
on supporting Black founders, 183–84
underestimated people and, 24, 25–26, 93
underrepresented communities and, 23–25, 36, 167, 170–74, 183–84
unicorn companies and, 119
visualization, 14
voting, power of, 118

Walmart, 85
wealth
access to, 61, 152

ABOUT THE AUTHOR

Arlan Hamilton built a venture capital fund from the
ground up, while homeless. She is the founder and managing partner of Backstage Capital, a fund that is dedicated
to minimizing disparities in tech by investing in high-
potential women, BIPOC, and LGBTQ+ founders. Since
its founding in 2015, Backstage Capital has raised $30 mil-
lion and has invested in more than two hundred start-ups.